GOD SPEAKS

LEARN HOW TO HEAR GOD

A JOURNEY THROUGH THE BOOK OF ACTS

Author
RICHARD MULL

Published by
LIGHT FORCE PUBLISHING

Cover design and layout: Jeff Damm Design

PRINTED IN THE UNITED STATES OF AMERICA

ISBN: 978-0-9778666-0-1

GOD SPEAKS
LEARN HOW TO HEAR GOD
A JOURNEY THROUGH THE BOOK OF ACTS

TABLE OF CONTENTS

GOD SPEAKS

LEARN HOW TO HEAR GOD

A JOURNEY THROUGH THE BOOK OF ACTS

SECTION

A

INTRODUCTION

GOD SPEAKS

LEARN HOW TO HEAR GOD

A JOURNEY THROUGH THE BOOK OF ACTS

OVERVIEW

Isaiah 52:6 Therefore **my people shall know my name**: therefore they shall know in that day that **I am he that doth speak**: behold, it is I. (underlining and emphasis added)

Isaiah 52:26 And said, "If you will diligently listen to the voice of the LORD your God, and will do that which is right in his sight, and will give ear to his commandments, and keep all his statutes, I will put none of these diseases on you, which I have brought on the Egyptians: for I am the LORD that heals you."

God Speaks The Book of Acts – The Acts of the Apostles is one book from the entire God Speaks Bible, but it is a profound book. It was chosen to be released first because it is the book that will most accurately reflect how God spoke during the New Testament church era. It is the book that relates the experience of the New Testament church age. God spoke through the book of Acts in every way that he spoke throughout history and then added a few new ways. The book is the most accurate reflection of how God speaks today, as if God might change how He communicates.

In the *God Speaks Study Bible* you will be impacted as you easily see and know when God himself is speaking as well as the various ways God uses to speak. What you will discover is that God is talking all the time, to all sorts of people, from all walks of life. You will see a myriad of different ways that God has spoken throughout time.

Our hope and prayer is that you will be inspired by the fact that God speaks and that He is no respecter of persons. We also trust that you will grow in your ability to hear God, when He is speaking to you.

Many believers have been taught that God stopped speaking when the Bible was canonized and that now He has chosen to limit His interaction with mankind to speaking through His written words the Bible. You can have a vibrant Christian walk, even if you only know God as He speaks through the Bible. But, how much more exciting it can be when you learn how to know God who in Isaiah 52:6 reveals Himself and His name as "I am He that doth speak."

Many believers who believe God can speak don't believe He has ever spoken to them or are not sure if He has. They have never been taught how to listen and hear and discern God's voice. May this Bible lead you into a vibrant new experience of hearing God as He speaks to you in very specific ways regarding His will, His love, His direction and His correction (yes, correction).

Below is a color coding guide. The symbols represent the various ways God speaks. The code is included in the header throughout the God Speaks Bible so that it can remind you of each different way God speaks. Familiarize yourself with the code before you start your journey through this exciting book.

TEXT COLOR LEGEND

	PURPLE	Is used when God is speaking directly in the first person.
	GREEN	Is used when a passage is talking about God speaking.
	GOLD	Is used when God is speaking through non-verbal communication.
	BROWN	Is used when Man is speaking on God's behalf in the Third Person.
	BLUE	Is used for Angels speaking on God's behalf or a vision or a dream.
	RED	These are the Words of Jesus.

GOD SPEAKS

LEARN HOW TO HEAR GOD

A JOURNEY THROUGH THE BOOK OF ACTS

LEARNING TO HEAR GOD'S VOICE

You can learn to hear God speak to you. He is talking all the time. He has probably been speaking to you your entire life. When people first learn to hear God's voice they often relate that they have heard God before many times but didn't know it was God speaking to them. He can speak today in any way that He spoke in the Bible and He hasn't limited Himself to certain ways of speaking.

There are many signs and wonders happening today that we fail to recognize. Even a lost world recognizes many signs today. Just listen to the conversations. People are talking about wars, tsunamis, famines, oil crises, economic challenges and more. Many people wonder aloud if God is trying to get our attention. Duh! When are we going to wake up that we are spiritual beings having a temporary physical experience. The natural phenomena around us are not arbitrary. God is always working.

Most people today have little or no understanding that they are primarily spiritual beings. God created us body, soul and spirit. There are hundreds of passages that mention our human spirit in the Bible and yet take a survey of your friends or your church. Ask the question, "Have you ever heard teaching about your human spirit?" Most of the time not one person will raise their hands. There are more passages about your human spirit than about the Holy Spirit. Hard to believe? Just look up the word spirit and read every passage in the Bible. You will find that most of the time it is talking about our human spirit.

God is spirit and He talks to our spirit, but we are so unaware of our spirit most of the time. When God speaks to us apart from the Word of God it is often to our spirit. Our mind often interprets what is in our spirit so sometimes we receive a message from God in our spirit and then we process that message in our mind and it can sound like our own thoughts. Most of my life I thought that hearing God would sound like the movies and TV where there is thunder rolling in the background and something like the voice of James Earl Jones rumbles in a deep base, "This is GOOODDDD." When I would ask God to speak to me I would have pictures in my mind and thoughts go through my mind. I thought these were distracting me from really hearing God. Little did I know that I was having visions and that my mind was interpreting things God was speaking to my spirit.

Jesus modeled for us a relationship with the Father that involved constant communication. We only know of one time where a voice came from heaven and that was at His baptism. Then there was the transfiguration where Moses and Elijah showed up. Yet, Jesus said, "…I do nothing of Myself; but as My Father hath taught Me, I speak these things." John 8:28 (KJ21)

We have a human spirit and God is spirit. It is vital that we learn to be aware of what the Holy Spirit is communicating with our human spirit God has placed within us.

There are dangers involved in hearing God's voice. Throughout time there have been false prophets, false dreams and visions, and lying signs and wonders. Satan himself used scripture to tempt Jesus. There is not one way of God's speaking that the enemy hasn't tried to copy and twist. Does that mean we stop trying to hear God's voice? Absolutely not.

Hearing God is like class 101 with Jesus. His sheep hear His voice. We must hear His voice if we want to follow the shepherd. In order to hear His voice it is important to be still and listen. I've heard God's voice in a room where the music was so loud, you couldn't hear yourself when you yelled. The still small voice was able to penetrate the noise without God even raising His voice. Noise can't drown out what our spirit hears and perceives. Paul perceived things in His Spirit from the Spirit of God. We can too.

GOD SPEAKS

LEARN HOW TO HEAR GOD

A JOURNEY THROUGH THE BOOK OF ACTS

INSTRUCTIONS TO LISTENING TO GOD

During this time each day take 10-20 minutes. If you have more time, then feel free to go as long as you want. During the next 4 weeks I encourage you to do this every day in a quiet place, if possible. God can speak to us over the noises of life, but for this time frame, seek out a quiet place and time, if possible. I encourage you as you listen to write everything down that goes through your mind and every image that comes into your head.

While you are listening don't censor what you write down. At the end of your time, ask God for discernment about what He is speaking and what is just your imagination or daydreaming or even demonic. Don't worry about making mistakes or getting this wrong. It is a learning exercise. You are not writing something to add to the Bible. Consider this a learning time.

Be sure to read the chapter in Acts every day and to check anything you believe God might be speaking to you through God's Word at the end of your time of listening.

Pay attention to any pictures that come to your mind. Whether they are moving images or vistas, write down every detail. They may be just colors or objects. Write down all the description you can of what you see. These are likely visions and have meaning that you can later ask God or even other believers to help you interpret. Don't get hung up in the moment on the meaning unless it comes to you.

If a song comes to mind, sing it (to yourself unless you are alone) and pay attention to the words. God may speak through a song. If a scripture reference comes to your mind write it down and look it up after your time of listening unless you are prompted to look it up right away.

Pay attention to what is happening in your spirit. Are you feeling peaceful or disturbed? What else are you feeling? Ask God to help you with this. He usually speaks to our spirit but we have such little awareness of our spirit that we process thing mostly in our minds. I explain this more in the daily lessons but from the beginning seek to be aware of your spirit and write down what comes to your spirit.

Whatever God asks you to do, if you are certain it is God, then obey Him. He might ask you to stop a habit, break off a relationship that is wrong, stop watching a TV show, or He might ask you to share your faith with someone, or speak a word of encouragement to total stranger. If you are listening, and you obey it will bless both of you. If you want to keep hearing him, I encourage you to obey Him.

Now, just listen!

There are more valuable resources online at www.operationlightforce.com regarding hearing God's voice. Including a DVD or CD set by Richard Mull entitled: Hearing God's Voice.

GOD SPEAKS

LEARN HOW TO HEAR GOD

A JOURNEY THROUGH THE BOOK OF ACTS

SECTION
1

WEEK 1 | LESSONS 1-7
STUDY GUIDE

GOD SPEAKS
LEARN HOW TO HEAR GOD
A JOURNEY THROUGH THE BOOK OF ACTS

WEEK 1 | LESSONS 1-7
GOD IS SPEAKING – CAN YOU HEAR HIM?

Today, many Christians cannot hear God speaking to them. Some say they have never heard God. Others say they have only heard God once or a few times in their life. Is that because God is not speaking? Or, is it because we are not listening or have not learned how to hear Him?

I believe that scripture teaches us that God has always been communicating with people and that if we are His children we should hear Him. God has spoken to every kind of person all throughout history. In Appendix 1 of this study you can see a list of who God spoke to in the book of Acts. If you were to see the entire list of people God spoke to in the Bible it would amaze you. God spoke to kings and rulers, both pagans and believers. He spoke to servants and slaves. He spoke to priests as well as warriors.

God has spoken in so many ways to so many people, it becomes clear that God loves to communicate and the variety of ways He uses is astounding. That is what this **God Speaks – Learning How to Hear God** journey is all about. I believe that if you seek Him you will find Him. You can hear Him and He is speaking. I pray that everyone who completes this study will be able to testify that they have heard God and that they have learned how to hear Him on a regular basis.

THE HOLLYWOOD SYNDROME

I often ask groups where I am speaking if they have a preconceived idea of what God sounds like. Almost without fail people raise their hands and blurt out the same names. Think about it for a moment. Have you had at any time a preconceived idea of what God would sound like when you hear Him? The answer is usually the same. People expect to hear a deep baritone or bass-sounding voice. I always expected a bit of thunder rolling in the background along with the voice. Ok, whose voices did you think of? The two names that often come up are James Earl Jones and Morgan Freeman. My next question is, has anyone ever heard the voice of either of these men when listening to God and the standard answer is laughter and head shakes to indicate a strong no.

I believe this is one of the most important journeys that everyone should take. Hearing God's voice is one of the most foundational components that Jesus taught us. Jesus even taught this by His own example. He said,

John 5:30 I can of my own self do nothing: as I hear, I judge: and my judgment is just; because I seek not my own will, but the will of the Father which has sent me.

John 8:28 Then said Jesus to them, When you have lifted up the Son of man, then shall you know that I am he, and that I do nothing of myself; but as my Father has taught me, I speak these things.

Jesus modeled to us a life of listening and obeying His Father's voice.

WILL SOMEONE LISTEN?

Now let's look at a passage that is very startling. It is a letter that Jesus dictated to John in a vision after he had died, resurrected and ascended to heaven. Many years later, Jesus came to John in a vision and told John to write 7 letters. This is his last letter to the church of Laodicea. Some teach that the letters not only were directed at the seven churches of the 7 cities they address but that they also address different ages of time and that Laodicea would comprise the latter days that we are living in. Let's read it:

Revelation 3:14 And to the angel of the church of the Laodiceans write; These things said the Amen, the faithful and true witness, the beginning of the creation of God; 15 I know your works, that you are neither cold nor hot: I would you were cold or hot. 16 So then because you are lukewarm, and neither cold nor hot, I will spew you out of my mouth. 17 Because you say, I am rich, and increased with goods, and have need of nothing; and know not that you are wretched, and miserable, and poor, and blind, and naked: 18 I counsel you to buy of me gold tried in the fire, that you may be rich; and white raiment, that you may be clothed, and that the shame of your nakedness do not appear; and anoint your eyes with eye salve, that you may see. 19 As many as I love, I rebuke and chasten: be zealous therefore, and repent. 20 Behold, I stand at the door, and knock: if any man hear my voice, and open the door, I will come in to him, and will sup with him, and he with me. 21 To him that overcomes will I grant to sit with me in my throne, even as I also overcame, and am set down with my Father in his throne. 22 He that has an ear, let him hear what the Spirit said to the churches. There is so much that this passage says that would be vital for us to discuss, but I want to focus on the last 3 verses so as to stay on task with the subject we are looking at in terms of hearing God's voice. Where is Jesus and what is he doing in verse 20?

If you said, He is standing at the door of someone's heart you are not alone but look again. Where is he standing? He is addressing the church. Jesus is standing at the door of the church, longing for someone to hear His voice and open the door so He can sit with him. How can we get to the place where God is standing on the outside longing to get in and be heard?

The passage ends in verse 22 with the way each of the letters ends, "He that has an ear, let him hear what the Spirit said to the churches." The NET Bible says it like this, "22 The one who has an ear had better hear what the Spirit says to the churches." It is not only what God said 2000 years ago that we must hear. We need to hear what the Spirit of God says to us today.

THE WRITTEN WORD OF GOD

I had been taught most of my life that God spoke to us through the written Word of God. I'll never forget moving and coming to a new church when I was 13 and some kids asking me what God had said to me lately. I looked at them like they had two heads. After a while I realized these kids read their Bibles and were serious about hearing God through scripture. It transformed my life as I began to read God's Word daily and it has continued throughout my life.

For the last 14 years I have been on a journey to hear God not only through the scriptures but also in any way He wants to communicate with me. We will journey together through a variety of ways God typically speaks as well as see some special ways He has spoken. You will be reading a chapter a day in Acts and will particularly be noticing the myriad of ways He spoke to people during the birth of the church. I believe many of you will experience more than one of those ways yourselves as we journey together.

THE BREAKDOWN

Let's take a look at where things began to break down. At creation the Spirit of God brooded over the earth, and Jesus was there and participated in creation as we are told in John 1 and Colossians 1. God walked with Adam and Eve in the Garden of Eden. Was that God the Father manifesting or was it the preincarnate Jesus? I don't know, but we know that God walked with and talked with mankind. Then Satan came as a serpent and the very first thing he attacked was God's voice and His Word. The serpent said, "Has God said?" or "Is it really true that God said?" The serpent attacked the words that God had spoken. Then we see the results beginning in verse 8:

Genesis 3:8-10 "And they heard the voice of the LORD God walking in the garden in the cool of the day: and Adam and his wife hid themselves from the presence of the LORD God amongst the trees of the garden. And the LORD God called unto Adam, and said unto him, Where art thou? And he said, I heard thy voice in the garden, and I was afraid, because I was naked; and I hid myself."

Adam and Eve, in their shame, hid from God when they heard His voice. Mankind has hidden from God's voice for a long time. If we are all truly honest, most of us are afraid of what the Lord might speak to us. Many expect that God is upset with us because of our sin and are afraid of His anger.

For many others, they fear God sending them somewhere far away to be a missionary and marry someone who is ugly and make them eat nothing but bread and water. One dear young man I know well was recently so excited about God speaking to Him through dreams and in visions until God started dealing with his idolatry of football and his poor treatment of his sisters. He commented, half joking, that God could stop talking to him now.

But isn't that true? We like to live our own way and make our own rules. If we let God in and listen, He might want to address some things in our lives that we want Him to leave well enough alone.

It is true; the Lord does rebuke those whom He loves. The Bible is very clear on that matter, but I find that He is so loving and tender and affirming. When we minister to people at Operation Light Force, we take time to listen to God with people. They are learning to hear God and, also, God speaks to us for them. Those are the most memorable and tender moments. People hardly ever ask me to email them the words that I say to them (though I like to think that I can be rather eloquent and affirming). However, almost every time, people want us to email them a copy of what God said to them, even when it is corrective in nature. They are so encouraged and testify that our time of listening to God was the most life-changing thing they have experienced.

HIS VOICE IS POWERFUL

Look at what the Psalmist wrote in Psalm 29 about the voice of the Lord:

Psalm 29: 3 "The voice of the LORD is on the waters: the God of glory thunders: the LORD is on many waters. 4 The voice of the LORD is powerful; the voice of the LORD is full of majesty. 5 The voice of the LORD breaks the cedars; yes, the LORD breaks the cedars of Lebanon. 6 He makes them also to skip like a calf; Lebanon and Sirion like a young unicorn. 7 The voice of the LORD divides the flames of fire. 8 The voice of the LORD shakes the wilderness; the LORD shakes the wilderness of Kadesh. 9 The voice

of the LORD makes the hinds to calve, and discovers the forests: and in his temple does everyone speak of his glory."

No wonder Hollywood makes God's voice out to be deep, resonant and accompanied with thunder. Moses and the children of Israel heard the thunder rolling when God spoke from Mount Sinai. God spoke in Genesis 1 and the universe came into existence. He spoke the planets into being. He spoke and there were the sun, moon and stars. He spoke and animals existed. Everything came into being at the sound of His voice.

Did God have to yell really loud to create everything? Is that what it means for His voice to be powerful? I have found that the still small voice of the Holy Spirit is so powerful and no one else in the room will hear what the Spirit speaks to me. I was once in a youth conference and the music was so loud you could hardly hear yourself. I heard the Lord's still small voice when I couldn't even hear my voice. He wasn't screaming either.

THE SHEPHERD'S VOICE

What did Jesus teach us about hearing God's voice? The most famous and incredible passage about God speaking is John 10.

John 10: 1 "Truly, truly, I say to you, He that enters not by the door into the sheepfold, but climbs up some other way, the same is a thief and a robber. 2 But he that enters in by the door is the shepherd of the sheep. 3 To him the porter opens; and the sheep hear his voice: and he calls his own sheep by name, and leads them out. 4 And when he puts forth his own sheep, he goes before them, and the sheep follow him: for they know his voice. 5 And a stranger will they not follow, but will flee from him: for they know not the voice of strangers."

Christ is the Shepherd and if we are children of His we are His sheep. It is so clear that the followers of Christ know His voice, yet many believers don't. I believe that there are many reasons that true believers are not able to hear God's voice. Actually, I believe that many have heard God's voice most of their lives and didn't know He was talking to them. That is what this journey will help you do. You will learn how to recognize the voice

	PURPLE	Is used when God is speaking directly in the first person.
	GREEN	Is used when a passage is talking about God speaking.
	GOLD	Is used when God is speaking through non-verbal communication.
	BROWN	Is used when Man is speaking on God's behalf in the Third Person.
	BLUE	Is used for Angels speaking on God's behalf or a vision or a dream.
	RED	These are the Words of Jesus.

ACTS: CHAPTER 1

1 The former treatise have I made, O Theophilus, of all that Jesus began both to do and teach,

2 Until the day in which he was taken up, after that he through the Holy Ghost had given commandments unto the apostles whom he had chosen:

3 To whom also he shewed himself alive after his passion by many infallible proofs, being seen of them forty days, and speaking of the things pertaining to the kingdom of God:

4 And, being assembled together with them, commanded them that they should not depart from Jerusalem, but wait for the promise of the Father, which, saith he, ye have heard of me.

5 For John truly baptized with water; but ye shall be baptized with the Holy Ghost not many days hence.

6 When they therefore were come together, they asked of him, saying, Lord, wilt thou at this time restore again the kingdom to Israel?

7 And he said unto them, It is not for you to know the times or the seasons, which the Father hath put in his own power.

8 But ye shall receive power, after that the Holy Ghost is come upon you: and ye shall be witnesses unto me both in Jerusalem, and in all Judaea, and in Samaria, and unto the uttermost part of the earth.

9 And when he had spoken these things, while they beheld, he was taken up; and a cloud received him out of their sight.

10 And while they looked steadfastly toward heaven as he went up, behold, two men stood by them in white apparel;

11 Which also said, Ye men of Galilee, why stand ye gazing up into heaven? this same Jesus, which is taken up from you into heaven, shall so come in like manner as ye have seen him go into heaven.

12 Then returned they unto Jerusalem from the mount called Olivet, which is from Jerusalem a sabbath day's journey.

13 And when they were come in, they went up into an upper room, where abode both Peter, and James, and John, and Andrew, Philip, and Thomas, Bartholomew, and Matthew, James the son of Alphaeus, and Simon Zelotes, and Judas the brother of James.

14 These all continued with one accord in prayer and supplication, with the women, and Mary the mother of Jesus, and with his brethren.

15 And in those days Peter stood up in the midst of the disciples, and said, (the number of names together were about an hundred and twenty,)

16 Men and brothers, this scripture must needs have been fulfilled, which the Holy Ghost by the mouth of David spoke before concerning Judas, which was guide to them that took Jesus.

17 For he was numbered with us, and had obtained part of this ministry.

18 Now this man purchased a field with the reward of iniquity; and falling headlong, he burst asunder in the middle, and all his bowels gushed out.

19 And it was known to all the dwellers at Jerusalem; so as that field is called in their proper tongue, Aceldama, that is to say, The field of blood.

ANGELS IN ACTS

Two angels speak when Jesus ascends into heaven (Acts 1:12-11)

An angel opens the prison doors for Peter (Acts 5:19-20)

References to angels appears in the Old Testament (Acts 7:35-38)

Reference to God's law being given by angels (Acts 7:53)

An angel gave Philip instructions (Acts 8:26)

An angel came to Cornelius in his vision (Acts 10:3-7)

An angel came to release Peter from Prison again (Acts 12:7-10)

An angel killed Herod because he failed to give God glory (Acts 12:23)

God spoke with Paul through an angel (Acts 28:23-25)

	PURPLE	Is used when God is speaking directly in the first person.
	GREEN	Is used when a passage is talking about God speaking.
	GOLD	Is used when God is speaking through non-verbal communication.
	BROWN	Is used when Man is speaking on God's behalf in the Third Person.
	BLUE	Is used for Angels speaking on God's behalf or a vision or a dream.
	RED	These are the Words of Jesus.

20 For it is written in the book of Psalms, Let his habitation be desolate, and let no man dwell therein: and his position as bishop let another take.

21 Why of these men which have companied with us all the time that the Lord Jesus went in and out among us,

22 Beginning from the baptism of John, to that same day that he was taken up from us, must one be ordained to be a witness with us of his resurrection.

23 And they appointed two, Joseph called Barsabas, who was surnamed Justus, and Matthias.

24 And they prayed, and said, You, Lord, which know the hearts of all men, show whether of these two you have chosen,

25 That he may take part of this ministry and apostleship, from which Judas by transgression fell, that he might go to his own place.

26 And they gave forth their lots; and the lot fell on Matthias; and he was numbered with the eleven apostles.

CASTING LOTS

God's way or chance? There is some biblical precedent for casting lots in decision when Israel was dividing the land in Joshua. When choosing between two good things this is fair. Some question whether Matthias was God's choice or whether Paul was?

PERSONAL NOTES

_____
_____
_____
_____
_____
_____
_____
_____
_____
_____
_____
_____
_____
_____
_____
_____
_____
_____
_____
_____
_____
_____
_____
_____
_____
_____
_____

DAY 1

DAILY LESSON

WEEK 1 | LESSON 1

SOME THINGS TO PONDER

1. What is the basis of Luke's writing this book or what is His source material (according to verses 1-4)?

_____

_____

2. What is unique about Jesus appearing and speaking in the beginning of the book of Acts as opposed to all throughout the gospels? (*Answer below*) _____

_____

_____

_____

3. Could Jesus appear today and speak to someone? Does He ever appear again to anyone in the Bible? _____

_____

_____

4. Have you ever seen an angel? _____

_____

Answer: In Acts, Jesus has resurrected from the dead.

LEARNING TO HEAR HIM - DAY 1 – MY SHEEP HEAR MY VOICE.

Hearing God's voice is the amazing privilege of God's children. It is a privilege, a right, a promise and a responsibility.

Jesus said, in John 10:27 "My sheep hear My voice, and I know them and they follow Me. 28 And I give unto them eternal life, and they shall never perish, neither shall any man pluck them out of My hand."

God spoke to every kind of person there is. He has spoken to kings, to pagans, to men and women. He has spoken to servants, prisoners, illegitimate children and those who despised Him. From cover to cover in the Bible, God is speaking to people. But there are also many who have never heard God's voice. Why is that?

Every single person can learn how to hear God's voice. That doesn't mean that all will. God loves all people and wants an intimate relationship with all mankind but unfortunately not everyone wants a relationship with Him. Others have never been taught how to hear God's voice.

What is astounding is that many of God's own children have never learned how to hear His voice. One of the greatest privileges and responsibilities we have has been sorely neglected. That is what this book and study are all about — teaching people how to hear and discern the voice of God.

DAY 1   DAILY LESSON

WEEK 1 | LESSON 1

LEARNING TO HEAR HIM - DAY 1 – MY SHEEP HEAR MY VOICE (CONTINUED)

Here are a few reasons why it is essential to know how to hear God's voice.

1. God wants to communicate with you.
2. You need His guidance – God has always guided His people and spoken specific directions when they would listen.
3. You need to know and do His will.
4. God wants to use you to minister to others.
5. No one else's opinion of you matters but His.

The list goes on and on.

Can you think of some more reasons it is worth making it a priority to listen to God? _____
_____
_____

NOTHING else matters as much. Do it! Take the time to listen.

Are you a child of God? Have you come to the place in your life where you asked Him to come into your heart and life and take control? Jesus used the analogy of sheep. Sheep follow the voice of their shepherd. If you haven't turned over the leadership of your life to God, then now would be a great time. Ask Him to forgive you of your sins, and ask the Lord to come in and take control of your life. He loves you and only has what is best for you in mind.

MAKING IT PERSONAL

1. Have you heard God before? How often? What was it/is it like for you? _____
_____

2. Do you believe that God wants to and will speak to you? Explain: _____
_____

3. Do you have any fears or concerns about listening for God's voice? What are they? _____
_____

4. Do you ever take time to listen for God? Is your schedule too busy for God? _____
_____

5. Do you have too many other voices and distractions in your life to pay attention to the Lord? _____
_____

DAY 1　DAILY LESSON

WEEK 1 | LESSON 1

TIME TO LISTEN

Write in the space below whatever God may be speaking to you. Don't censor it as you write. If a song comes to mind pay attention to the words and write them. If scripture, write down the reference or the verse, if random thoughts write them. If you see images in your mind write them. Afterward ask God for discernment as to what each thing means. If you do not think you hear anything at first - be patient - it might take a few minutes. Pray, "Lord please help me focus my thoughts on you." If a person, place or thing comes to mind, ask God, "Is there something you would like to say about this?"

DAY 2

PURPLE	Is used when God is speaking directly in the first person.
GREEN	Is used when a passage is talking about God speaking.
GOLD	Is used when God is speaking through non-verbal communication.
BROWN	Is used when Man is speaking on God's behalf in the Third Person.
BLUE	Is used for Angels speaking on God's behalf or a vision or a dream.
RED	These are the Words of Jesus.

ACTS: CHAPTER 2

1 And when the day of Pentecost was fully come, they were all with one accord in one place.

2 And suddenly there came a sound from heaven as of a rushing mighty wind, and it filled all the house where they were sitting.

3 And there appeared to them cloven tongues like as of fire, and it sat on each of them.

4 And they were all filled with the Holy Ghost, and began to speak with other tongues, as the Spirit gave them utterance.

5 And there were dwelling at Jerusalem Jews, devout men, out of every nation under heaven.

6 Now when this was noised abroad, the multitude came together, and were confounded, because that every man heard them speak in his own language.

7 And they were all amazed and marveled, saying one to another, Behold, are not all these which speak Galilaeans?

8 And how hear we every man in our own tongue, wherein we were born?

9 Parthians, and Medes, and Elamites, and the dwellers in Mesopotamia, and in Judaea, and Cappadocia, in Pontus, and Asia,

10 Phrygia, and Pamphylia, in Egypt, and in the parts of Libya about Cyrene, and strangers of Rome, Jews and proselytes,

11 Cretes and Arabians, we do hear them speak in our tongues the wonderful works of God.

12 And they were all amazed, and were in doubt, saying one to another, What means this?

13 Others mocking said, These men are full of new wine.

14 But Peter, standing up with the eleven, lifted up his voice, and said to them, You men of Judaea, and all you that dwell at Jerusalem, be this known to you, and listen to my words:

15 For these are not drunken, as you suppose, seeing it is but the third hour of the day.

16 But this is that which was spoken by the prophet Joel;

17 And it shall come to pass in the last days, said God, I will pour out of my Spirit on all flesh: and your sons and your daughters shall prophesy, and your young men shall see visions, and your old men shall dream dreams:

18 And on my servants and on my handmaidens I will pour out in those days of my Spirit; and they shall prophesy:

19 And I will show wonders in heaven above, and signs in the earth beneath; blood, and fire, and vapor of smoke:

20 The sun shall be turned into darkness, and the moon into blood, before the great and notable day of the Lord come:

21 And it shall come to pass, that whoever shall call on the name of the Lord shall be saved.

22 You men of Israel, hear these words; Jesus of Nazareth, a man approved of God among you by miracles and wonders and signs, which God did by him in the middle of you, as you yourselves also know:

23 Him, being delivered by the determinate counsel and foreknowledge of God, you have taken, and by wicked hands have crucified and slain:

24 Whom God has raised up, having loosed the pains of death: because it was not possible that he should be held of it.

25 For David speaks concerning him, I foresaw the Lord always before my face, for he is on my right hand, that I should not be moved:

SUPERNATURAL GOD

—From the beginning of time God has displayed Himself through supernatural means to reveal Himself to the world. He doesn't play by our rules. He defies nature. In Acts 2 God sends the sound from heaven of wind, puts fire on the heads of those gathered and speaks through people in languages they don't know.

DAY 2

	PURPLE	Is used when God is speaking directly in the first person.
	GREEN	Is used when a passage is talking about God speaking.
	GOLD	Is used when God is speaking through non-verbal communication.
	BROWN	Is used when Man is speaking on God's behalf in the Third Person.
	BLUE	Is used for Angels speaking on God's behalf or a vision or a dream.
	RED	These are the Words of Jesus.

26 Therefore did my heart rejoice, and my tongue was glad; moreover also my flesh shall rest in hope:

27 Because you will not leave my soul in hell, neither will you suffer your Holy One to see corruption.

28 You have made known to me the ways of life; you shall make me full of joy with your countenance.

29 Men and brothers, let me freely speak to you of the patriarch David, that he is both dead and buried, and his sepulcher is with us to this day.

30 Therefore being a prophet, and knowing that God had sworn with an oath to him, that of the fruit of his loins, according to the flesh, he would raise up Christ to sit on his throne;

31 He seeing this before spoke of the resurrection of Christ, that his soul was not left in hell, neither his flesh did see corruption.

32 This Jesus has God raised up, whereof we all are witnesses.

33 Therefore being by the right hand of God exalted, and having received of the Father the promise of the Holy Ghost, he has shed forth this, which you now see and hear.

34 For David is not ascended into the heavens: but he said himself, The Lord said to my Lord, Sit you on my right hand,

35 Until I make your foes your footstool.

36 Therefore let all the house of Israel know assuredly, that God has made the same Jesus, whom you have crucified, both Lord and Christ.

37 Now when they heard this, they were pricked in their heart, and said to Peter and to the rest of the apostles, Men and brothers, what shall we do?

38 Then Peter said to them, Repent, and be baptized everyone of you in the name of Jesus Christ for the remission of sins, and you shall receive the gift of the Holy Ghost.

39 For the promise is to you, and to your children, and to all that are afar off, even as many as the LORD our God shall call.

40 And with many other words did he testify and exhort, saying, Save yourselves from this untoward generation.

41 Then they that gladly received his word were baptized: and the same day there were added to them about three thousand souls.

42 And they continued steadfastly in the apostles' doctrine and fellowship, and in breaking of bread, and in prayers.

43 And fear came on every soul: and many wonders and signs were done by the apostles.

44 And all that believed were together, and had all things common;

45 And sold their possessions and goods, and parted them to all men, as every man had need.

46 And they, continuing daily with one accord in the temple, and breaking bread from house to house, did eat their meat with gladness and singleness of heart,

47 Praising God, and having favor with all the people. And the Lord added to the church daily such as should be saved.

GOD SPEAKS THROUGH OLD TESTAMENT

– Acts 1:16; 2:16-20, 2:30-34; 3:18, 21-25; 7:2-3, 30-38, 42-43; 13:32-35, 44-49; 15:15-17; 25:6-7; 26:22-23 The apostles used the Old Testament text when they spoke. They did not treat it as obsolete or invalid. Instead it was their authoritative source for truth. Some teach that the Old Testament is done away with, but the New helps define the Old. Both make our faith full.

PERSONAL NOTES

_____

_____

_____

_____

_____

_____

DAY 2

DAILY LESSON

WEEK 1 | LESSON 2

MIRACLES, SIGNS AND WONDERS

Sound of rushing wind (Acts 2:2)

Tongues of fire (Acts 2:2-4)

Speaking in tongues (Acts 2:8-11)

Many wonders and signs done by apostles (Acts 2:43)

God healed a lame man (Acts 4:22, 30)

Peter and John heal the sick (Acts 4:30-31)

Apostles healed many sick (Acts 5:12)

Peter was used to heal the sick even by his shadow (Acts 5:15-16)

Steven healed the sick and did miracles (Acts 6:8)

God spoke through the burning bush in the Old Testament (Acts 7:30-34)

Philip did miracles, healed the sick and cast out demons (Acts 8:6-7)

Paul and Barnabas preach accompanied with signs and wonders. (Acts 14:3)

Judas and Silas had message confirmed (Acts 15:32)

An earthquake opened the prison for Paul and Silas (Acts 16:26)

God spoke to us through the resurrection of Jesus (Acts 17:31)

SOME THINGS TO PONDER

1. How many unique ways can you find in this chapter of Acts that God spoke or did to reveal Himself?

   _____

   _____

   _____

2. When Jesus told them to wait in Jerusalem until they were filled with the Holy Spirit, do you think any of them imagined this scene? What do you think? _____

   _____

   _____

3. Has God ever worked in a way that surprised you and was outside of your expectations and experience?

   _____

   _____

4. This entire scene is wild and exciting. Wind from heaven, tongues of fire on people's heads, people speaking in other languages, people thinking the Christians are drunk, Peter preaching in the open air, signs and wonders happening, people sharing their possessions and meeting house to house. Does this sound like your experience with God? Why or Why Not? _____

   _____

   _____

5. If your experience of God is vastly different from what you read in Acts and the Gospels, what are some possible reasons? _____

   _____

   _____

LEARNING TO HEAR HIM - DAY 2 - LIMITING BELIEFS AND UNLEARNING

Proverbs 8:34 Blessed is the man who listens to me, watching daily at my gates, waiting at my doorposts.

To begin with, you have to deal with anything you have been taught that does not line up with God's Word. If you have been taught that God stopped speaking and you believe that, then you are at a huge disadvantage. In the same way Jesus could not convince the religious leaders of His day that their understanding of the Messiah was wrong. If we have deeply held beliefs that we believe are biblical but don't truly line up with scripture, then often times we will fight to hold onto those beliefs.

One example of this type of belief that many have had and taught to others is that when the Bible was finished God had said all He needed to say and that the Bible was everything that we need. This teaching is primarily based upon Revelation 22:18 where John is writing the words of God Himself Who says, "If any man shall add unto these things, God will add unto him the plagues that are written in this book."

The teaching that God only speaks through the Bible is built upon this verse in Revelation as well as a verse in 1 Corinthians 13:10 that says, "But when that which is perfect is come, then that which is in part shall be done away." The conclusion is that the "perfect" refers to the Bible and that all other means of God speaking, like prophecy and tongues and signs and wonders, are not necessary any more. They teach that the warning mentioned in Revelation means that God will not speak anything else.

If you hold to this deeply then there would be a measure of fear involved in ever saying, "God spoke to me." If God speaking today is a contradiction of Revelation 22:18 then you are inviting the plagues on you and that is a scary thing. People who teach this and believe this hold the scripture in high regard and are sincere believers. I was taught this and accepted it for a long time.

First of all, it is very bad to build your biblical belief system on just a few verses. If we are going to learn what God is like and what the Bible teaches us on any subject we need to look at all of scripture. We must let scripture interpret scripture. Are there other passages that tell us that the God who has communicated with people all throughout time in a personal manner is going to stop speaking when the Bible is completed? The answer is no. If you hold the belief that God has stopped speaking personally to people today, I encourage you to study God's Word thoroughly to make sure this is what the Bible teaches.

As we can see in the book of Acts alone, God is speaking all the time. And, He is talking to all kinds of people, both believers and unbelievers. God loves to communicate.

Second, to say that God put everything He had to say into one book and stopped communicating doesn't seem make logical sense. Why would such a personal God who created us and spent most of history talking to all kinds of people suddenly, around the birth of the church, stop talking to His bride, or to anyone else, for that matter?

I have written other books that I believe are totally worth reading. I believe that God inspired them but I don't want anyone to think that the books I wrote should be added to the Bible. I love it when people come to me and says that they read my book. I don't respond to them by saying that everything I have to say is written in that book and I don't have anything else to say to them. Yes, they will get to know me better if they read my book but it is even better to spend time with me. Why would God all of a sudden stop communicating and say, "It's all in my book." He may want us to read the book first as well as be with Him and listen to Him but not instead of doing these things.

DAY 2

WEEK 1 | LESSON 2

DAILY LESSON

MAKING IT PERSONAL

1. What have you been taught about God speaking? _____
_____
_____

2. What have you believed about God speaking to you? _____
_____
_____

3. Can you see why any of your beliefs could limit your ability to listen to and hear God clearly?
_____
_____

4. What do you think about all the creative and unique ways you have seen God speaking in Acts so far?
_____
_____

TIME TO LISTEN

Write in the space below whatever God may be speaking to you. Don't censor it as you write. If a song comes to mind pay attention to the words and write them. If scripture, write down the reference or the verse, if random thoughts write them. If you see images in your mind write them. Afterward ask God for discernment as to what each thing means.

_____
_____
_____
_____
_____
_____
_____
_____
_____
_____
_____
_____

PURPLE	Is used when God is speaking directly in the first person.	
GREEN	Is used when a passage is talking about God speaking.	
GOLD	Is used when God is speaking through non-verbal communication.	
BROWN	Is used when Man is speaking on God's behalf in the Third Person.	
BLUE	Is used for Angels speaking on God's behalf or a vision or a dream.	
RED	These are the Words of Jesus.	

ACTS 3 CHAPTER 3

1 Now Peter and John went up together into the temple at the hour of prayer, being the ninth hour.

2 And a certain man lame from his mother's womb was carried, whom they laid daily at the gate of the temple which is called Beautiful, to ask alms of them that entered into the temple;

3 Who seeing Peter and John about to go into the temple asked an alms.

4 And Peter, fastening his eyes on him with John, said, Look on us.

5 And he gave heed to them, expecting to receive something of them.

6 Then Peter said, Silver and gold have I none; but such as I have give I you: In the name of Jesus Christ of Nazareth rise up and walk.

7 And he took him by the right hand, and lifted him up: and immediately his feet and ankle bones received strength.

8 And he leaping up stood, and walked, and entered with them into the temple, walking, and leaping, and praising God.

9 And all the people saw him walking and praising God:

10 And they knew that it was he which sat for alms at the Beautiful gate of the temple: and they were filled with wonder and amazement at that which had happened to him.

11 And as the lame man which was healed held Peter and John, all the people ran together to them in the porch that is called Solomon's, greatly wondering.

12 And when Peter saw it, he answered to the people, You men of Israel, why marvel you at this? or why look you so earnestly on us, as though by our own power or holiness we had made this man to walk?

13 The God of Abraham, and of Isaac, and of Jacob, the God of our fathers, has glorified his Son Jesus; whom you delivered up, and denied him in the presence of Pilate, when he was determined to let him go.

14 But you denied the Holy One and the Just, and desired a murderer to be granted to you;

15 And killed the Prince of life, whom God has raised from the dead; whereof we are witnesses.

16 And his name through faith in his name has made this man strong, whom you see and know: yes, the faith which is by him has given him this perfect soundness in the presence of you all.

17 And now, brothers, I know that through ignorance you did it, as did also your rulers.

18 But those things, which God before had showed by the mouth of all his prophets, that Christ should suffer, he has so fulfilled.

19 Repent you therefore, and be converted, that your sins may be blotted out, when the times of refreshing shall come from the presence of the Lord.

20 And he shall send Jesus Christ, which before was preached to you:

21 Whom the heaven must receive until the times of restitution of all things, which God has spoken by the mouth of all his holy prophets since the world began.

22 For Moses truly said to the fathers, A prophet shall the Lord your God raise up to you of your brothers, like to me; him shall you hear in all things whatever he shall say to you.

23 And it shall come to pass, that every soul, which will not hear that prophet, shall be destroyed from among the people.

24 Yes, and all the prophets from Samuel and those that follow after, as many as have spoken, have likewise foretold of these days.

25 You are the children of the prophets, and of the covenant which God made with our fathers, saying to Abraham, And in your seed shall all the kindreds of the earth be blessed.

26 To you first God, having raised up his Son Jesus, sent him to bless you, in turning away everyone of you from his iniquities.

DAY 3

DAILY LESSON

SOME THINGS TO PONDER

1. What did Peter and John have to offer to the lame man? _____

   _____

2. Did the apostles show any hesitation or doubt about what God was going to do for this man? How did they know? _____

   _____

3. What impact did this miracle have upon all the people who looked on? _____

   _____

4. What do miracles like this demonstrate about God? _____

   _____

LEARNING TO HEAR GOD - DAY THREE – WOULD GOD REALLY TALK TO ME?

Take a minute to look at the list of people that God spoke to in Acts. (Appendix II- Page 162) It is amazing to see how many people God spoke to as well as the myriad of ways that He speaks.

The reason that it is important to look at that list is that many people don't believe that God would speak to them. They believe God speaks and that He could speak but they don't believe that they are important enough for God to speak to them personally.

When we look at the list of who God speaks to in Acts and throughout the entire Bible, it is astonishing. It is amazing! God is talking all the time and to people from all walks of life.

Nowhere does God limit Himself to talking only to important people, saints, leaders, or any other limitation. We can get to feeling like we are not important enough for God, but that is a lie that is definitely not what the Lord has to say about us.

Throughout the Bible God spoke to servants and to kings. He spoke to His Patriarchs as well as to pagan kings. He spoke in hundreds of different and unique ways.

Sure, there are certain ways that God normally speaks throughout the Bible, from prophets to scripture to dreams and visions. But, God is as creative as can be. In Daniel God sends a hand to write on a wall. In Deuteronomy, he allows a donkey to talk. In Acts, He puts tongues of fire on everyone's head. Pretty creative, isn't He?

Yes! God can speak to you and wants to speak to you, and it can be part of your normal daily experience if you will listen and believe.

DAY 3

DAILY LESSON

MAKING IT PERSONAL

1. Do you struggle with believing God would talk to you? Why? _____
   _____
   _____

2. What is the most interesting way you have heard of someone today sharing of how they heard God?
   _____
   _____
   _____

3. Is there a certain way that God spoke in the Bible, or with what you have read so far, that you would like for him to speak to you, in your life? _____
   _____
   _____

TIME TO LISTEN

Write in the space below whatever God may be speaking to you. Don't censor it as you write. If a song comes to mind pay attention to the words and write them. If scripture, write down the reference or the verse, if random thoughts write them. If you see images in your mind write them. Afterward ask God for discernment as to what each thing means. _____
_____
_____
_____
_____
_____
_____
_____
_____
_____
_____
_____
_____
_____
_____
_____
_____
_____

DAY 4

WEEK 1 | LESSON 4

	PURPLE	Is used when God is speaking directly in the first person.
	GREEN	Is used when a passage is talking about God speaking.
	GOLD	Is used when God is speaking through non-verbal communication.
	BROWN	Is used when Man is speaking on God's behalf in the Third Person.
	BLUE	Is used for Angels speaking on God's behalf or a vision or a dream.
	RED	These are the Words of Jesus.

ACTS CHAPTER 4

1 And as they spoke to the people, the priests, and the captain of the temple, and the Sadducees, came on them,

2 Being grieved that they taught the people, and preached through Jesus the resurrection from the dead.

3 And they laid hands on them, and put them in hold to the next day: for it was now eventide.

4 However, many of them which heard the word believed; and the number of the men was about five thousand.

5 And it came to pass on the morrow, that their rulers, and elders, and scribes,

6 And Annas the high priest, and Caiaphas, and John, and Alexander, and as many as were of the kindred of the high priest, were gathered together at Jerusalem.

7 And when they had set them in the middle, they asked, By what power, or by what name, have you done this?

8 Then Peter, filled with the Holy Ghost, said to them, You rulers of the people, and elders of Israel,

9 If we this day be examined of the good deed done to the weak man, by what means he is made whole;

10 Be it known to you all, and to all the people of Israel, that by the name of Jesus Christ of Nazareth, whom you crucified, whom God raised from the dead, even by him does this man stand here before you whole.

11 This is the stone which was set at nothing of you builders, which is become the head of the corner.

12 Neither is there salvation in any other: for there is none other name under heaven given among men, whereby we must be saved.

13 Now when they saw the boldness of Peter and John, and perceived that they were unlearned and ignorant men, they marveled; and they took knowledge of them, that they had been with Jesus.

14 And beholding the man which was healed standing with them, they could say nothing against it.

15 But when they had commanded them to go aside out of the council, they conferred among themselves,

WHAT ARE SIGNS & WONDERS? HOW DO THEY DIFFER?

Signs, wonders, and miracles demonstrate the power and character of God in various ways. Signs are miraculous events that happen on earth that demonstrate God's power and character. Wonders are miraculous events that happen in the heavenly realm that show the power and character of God.

16 Saying, What shall we do to these men? for that indeed a notable miracle has been done by them is manifest to all them that dwell in Jerusalem; and we cannot deny it.

17 But that it spread no further among the people, let us straightly threaten them, that they speak from now on to no man in this name.

18 And they called them, and commanded them not to speak at all nor teach in the name of Jesus.

19 But Peter and John answered and said to them, Whether it be right in the sight of God to listen to you more than to God, judge you.

20 For we cannot but speak the things which we have seen and heard.

21 So when they had further threatened them, they let them go, finding nothing how they might punish them, because of the people: for all men glorified God for that which was done.

22 For the man was above forty years old, on whom this miracle of healing was showed.

23 And being let go, they went to their own company, and reported all that the chief priests and elders had said to them.

24 And when they heard that, they lifted up their voice to God with one accord, and said, Lord, you are God, which have made heaven, and earth, and the sea, and all that in them is:

DAY 4

	PURPLE	Is used when God is speaking directly in the first person.
	GREEN	Is used when a passage is talking about God speaking.
	GOLD	Is used when God is speaking through non-verbal communication.
	BROWN	Is used when Man is speaking on God's behalf in the Third Person.
	BLUE	Is used for Angels speaking on God's behalf or a vision or a dream.
	RED	These are the Words of Jesus.

25 Who by the mouth of your servant David have said, Why did the heathen rage, and the people imagine vain things?

26 The kings of the earth stood up, and the rulers were gathered together against the Lord, and against his Christ.

27 For of a truth against your holy child Jesus, whom you have anointed, both Herod, and Pontius Pilate, with the Gentiles, and the people of Israel, were gathered together,

28 For to do whatever your hand and your counsel determined before to be done.

29 And now, Lord, behold their threatenings: and grant to your servants, that with all boldness they may speak your word,

30 By stretching forth your hand to heal; and that signs and wonders may be done by the name of your holy child Jesus.

31 And when they had prayed, the place was shaken where they were assembled together; and they were all filled with the Holy Ghost, and they spoke the word of God with boldness.

32 And the multitude of them that believed were of one heart and of one soul: neither said any of them that ought of the things which he possessed was his own; but they had all things common.

33 And with great power gave the apostles witness of the resurrection of the Lord Jesus: and great grace was on them all.

34 Neither was there any among them that lacked: for as many as were possessors of lands or houses sold them, and brought the prices of the things that were sold,

35 And laid them down at the apostles' feet: and distribution was made to every man according as he had need.

36 And Joses, who by the apostles was surnamed Barnabas, (which is, being interpreted, The son of consolation,) a Levite, and of the country of Cyprus,

37 Having land, sold it, and brought the money, and laid it at the apostles' feet.

SPEAKING BY THE HOLY SPIRIT

There are times when we are faced with a situation and must respond with an answer we cannot give. God sent His Holy Spirit to guide us and give us words when we need them. Have you ever felt like the words coming out of your mouth were not your own, but God speaking? Here in Acts 4 Peter had God speak through him.

PERSONAL NOTES

_____
_____
_____
_____
_____
_____
_____
_____
_____
_____
_____
_____
_____
_____
_____
_____
_____
_____
_____
_____
_____
_____

DAY 4

DAILY LESSON

WEEK 1 | LESSON 4

SOME THINGS TO PONDER

1. What did Peter and John do that made the spiritual leaders so upset (verse 2)? _____
_____
_____

2. What were some of the evidences that this miracle of healing was real? Why did these men not believe?
_____
_____

3. What sign occurred in this passage? What purpose would a sign like this serve? _____
_____
_____

4. Has God ever used a sign in your life to confirm His will or to give you direction or for another purpose?
_____
_____

LEARNING TO HEAR GOD - DAY 4 – IT'S NOT LIKE HOLLYWOOD

I remember when I first started listening to God, I had a preconceived idea of what it would be like to hear God. I'm convinced it came from the movies or TV. I was certain that it would start with a bolt of lightning and the sound of rolling thunder and that a deep resonant voice like that of James Earl Jones would sound from heaven.

It was very frustrating to have pictures running through my head and I thought they were just distractions in my mind. I had no idea God was giving me visions. I had no idea that God was speaking to me and that my thoughts were in reality what I was hearing Him say. I will explain this better in another session but let me just say that my preconceived ideas were keeping me from recognizing God's voice.

The movies had painted for us an image of God speaking that keeps us from hearing God. What are your preconceived ideas? If you know God's voice, do you remember a time before you heard God and what you believed it would be like?

DAILY LESSON

It is important for us to put our preconceived ideas to the test of scripture. There are very few times that God had thunder and lightning accompanying His voice. It is just about as rare that we are told that an audible voice came from heaven. Often we can read a passage about God speaking to someone and assume that he heard a voice from heaven, but that is not necessarily the case.

Often we are not told clearly how the person experienced hearing God's voice. It is going to be important as we lay a foundation for hearing God that our preconceived ideas get left outside so that we can build upon a clean foundation and understand what the Bible really says about God speaking and God's voice.

Recently in speaking to a group of teens I asked if any had a preconceived idea of what God's voice sounded like and half the group could identify a voice. At the top of the list were James Earl Jones and Morgan Freeman. One said Leonard Nimoy. Others said a deep, resonant voice. How about you?

MAKING IT PERSONAL

1. What have you believed in the past about how God would speak to you, when He would speak?
   _____
   _____
   _____

2. Are you open to God speaking to you in ways other than what you have expected? _____
   _____
   _____
   _____

3. How much is Hollywood (movies & TV) a part of your life? How much do you think it affects your thoughts, beliefs, etc.? _____
   _____
   _____

DAY 4

WEEK 1 | LESSON 4

DAILY LESSON

Write in the space below whatever God may be speaking to you. Don't censor it as you write. If a song comes to mind pay attention to the words and write them. If scripture, write down the reference or the verse, if random thoughts write them. If you see images in your mind write them. Afterward ask God for discernment as to what each thing means.

DAY 5

PURPLE	Is used when God is speaking directly in the first person.	
GREEN	Is used when a passage is talking about God speaking.	
GOLD	Is used when God is speaking through non-verbal communication.	
BROWN	Is used when Man is speaking on God's behalf in the Third Person.	
BLUE	Is used for Angels speaking on God's behalf or a vision or a dream.	
RED	These are the Words of Jesus.	

ACTS CHAPTER 5

1 But a certain man named Ananias, with Sapphira his wife, sold a possession,

2 And kept back part of the price, his wife also being privy to it, and brought a certain part, and laid it at the apostles' feet.

3 But Peter said, Ananias, why has Satan filled your heart to lie to the Holy Ghost, and to keep back part of the price of the land?

4 Whiles it remained, was it not your own? and after it was sold, was it not in your own power? why have you conceived this thing in your heart? you have not lied to men, but to God.

5 And Ananias hearing these words fell down, and gave up the ghost: and great fear came on all them that heard these things.

6 And the young men arose, wound him up, and carried him out, and buried him.

7 And it was about the space of three hours after, when his wife, not knowing what was done, came in.

8 And Peter answered to her, Tell me whether you sold the land for so much? And she said, Yes, for so much.

9 Then Peter said to her, How is it that you have agreed together to tempt the Spirit of the Lord? behold, the feet of them which have buried your husband are at the door, and shall carry you out.

10 Then fell she down straightway at his feet, and yielded up the ghost: and the young men came in, and found her dead, and, carrying her forth, buried her by her husband.

11 And great fear came on all the church, and on as many as heard these things.

12 And by the hands of the apostles were many signs and wonders worked among the people; (and they were all with one accord in Solomon's porch.

13 And of the rest dared no man join himself to them: but the people magnified them.

14 And believers were the more added to the Lord, multitudes both of men and women.)

HOLY GHOST WITNESSES

The apostles were telling people what they knew to be true but so was the Holy Ghost. God is witnessing to people and drawing people to Himself. (Acts 5:32)

ANGELIC COMMISSIONING

In Acts 5:19 an angel commissions the apostles after releasing them from prison. The angel told them to "Go, stand and speak in the temple...all the words of this life." This is what they had just been imprisoned for.

15 So that they brought forth the sick into the streets, and laid them on beds and couches, that at the least the shadow of Peter passing by might overshadow some of them.

16 There came also a multitude out of the cities round about to Jerusalem, bringing sick folks, and them which were vexed with unclean spirits: and they were healed everyone.

17 Then the high priest rose up, and all they that were with him, (which is the sect of the Sadducees,) and were filled with indignation,

18 And laid their hands on the apostles, and put them in the common prison.

19 But the angel of the Lord by night opened the prison doors, and brought them forth, and said,

20 Go, stand and speak in the temple to the people all the words of this life.

21 And when they heard that, they entered into the temple early in the morning, and taught. But the high priest came, and they that were with him, and called the council together, and all the senate of the children of Israel, and sent to the prison to have them brought.

22 But when the officers came, and found them not in the prison, they returned and told,

	PURPLE	Is used when God is speaking directly in the first person.
	GREEN	Is used when a passage is talking about God speaking.
	GOLD	Is used when God is speaking through non-verbal communication.
	BROWN	Is used when Man is speaking on God's behalf in the Third Person.
	BLUE	Is used for Angels speaking on God's behalf or a vision or a dream.
	RED	These are the Words of Jesus.

23 Saying, The prison truly found we shut with all safety, and the keepers standing without before the doors: but when we had opened, we found no man within.

24 Now when the high priest and the captain of the temple and the chief priests heard these things, they doubted of them whereunto this would grow.

25 Then came one and told them, saying, Behold, the men whom you put in prison are standing in the temple, and teaching the people.

26 Then went the captain with the officers, and brought them without violence: for they feared the people, lest they should have been stoned.

27 And when they had brought them, they set them before the council: and the high priest asked them,

28 Saying, Did not we straitly command you that you should not teach in this name? and, behold, you have filled Jerusalem with your doctrine, and intend to bring this man's blood on us.

29 Then Peter and the other apostles answered and said, We ought to obey God rather than men.

30 The God of our fathers raised up Jesus, whom you slew and hanged on a tree.

31 Him has God exalted with his right hand to be a Prince and a Savior, for to give repentance to Israel, and forgiveness of sins.

32 And we are his witnesses of these things; and so is also the Holy Ghost, whom God has given to them that obey him.

33 When they heard that, they were cut to the heart, and took counsel to slay them.

34 Then stood there up one in the council, a Pharisee, named Gamaliel, a doctor of the law, had in reputation among all the people, and commanded to put the apostles forth a little space;

35 And said to them, You men of Israel, take heed to yourselves what you intend to do as touching these men.

36 For before these days rose up Theudas, boasting himself to be somebody; to whom a number of men, about four hundred, joined themselves: who was slain; and all, as many as obeyed him, were scattered, and brought to nothing.

37 After this man rose up Judas of Galilee in the days of the taxing, and drew away much people after him: he also perished; and all, even as many as obeyed him, were dispersed.

38 And now I say to you, Refrain from these men, and let them alone: for if this counsel or this work be of men, it will come to nothing:

39 But if it be of God, you cannot overthrow it; lest haply you be found even to fight against God.

40 And to him they agreed: and when they had called the apostles, and beaten them, they commanded that they should not speak in the name of Jesus, and let them go.

41 And they departed from the presence of the council, rejoicing that they were counted worthy to suffer shame for his name.

42 And daily in the temple, and in every house, they ceased not to teach and preach Jesus Christ.

PERSONAL NOTES

_____

_____

_____

_____

_____

_____

_____

_____

_____

_____

_____

_____

_____

_____

_____

_____

_____

DAY 5

WEEK 1 | LESSON 5

DAILY LESSON

SOME THINGS TO PONDER

1. This chapter begins with a difficult story of Ananias and Sapphira. What purpose does this story and sign serve for us? _____
_____
_____

2. According to verses 12-16 the apostles were doing many signs and miracles. What purposes of God are served when miracles and signs occur? _____
_____
_____

3. Why do you think God sent His message through an angel in verses 18-19? Have you ever gotten direction or any word from God by an angel? _____
_____
_____

4. What role did Peter attribute to the Holy Spirit in verses 29-32? _____
_____

LEARNING TO HEAR GOD - DAY 5 – BE A BEREAN

God speaks through the Bible. This needs to be clearly stated. Some today believe that the only relevant biblical material that we should spend our time reading and understanding is the New Testament. Others believe that to test our beliefs or someone's teaching by scripture is too narrow-minded. This wasn't true of the early church. They quoted scripture and studied scripture and tested the things they were being taught by how it lined up with scripture.

When Paul the apostle came to Berea in Acts 17:10-11, he said that the people of Berea were more noble than those in Thessalonica because they searched the scriptures to make sure that what Paul was saying was true. Paul was encouraging us to be like the people of Berea and not just accept any new teaching because it sounds good or interesting.

The Bible, God's Word, is the standard that we must use to test everything we hear. That means that to hear God well, and be able to discern whether what we hear is true, we must know God's Word and we must know it well.

I was with a man once in a federal prison, ministering, who had believed that God the Father, the Son, and the Holy Spirit had told him to kill his parents. Now that is easy to judge from scripture, and most people wouldn't even believe that God had told him that.

DAY 5

DAILY LESSON

WEEK 1 | LESSON 5

When we don't have a firm foundation, like God's Word, for our decision making we become vulnerable to all sorts of teaching that can actually be destructive.

Satan himself actually used the Bible when he confronted Jesus in Luke 4. So just because people open the Bible, quote the Bible or say they believe and teach the Bible doesn't mean what they say is true. What I mean is that scripture can be misused, mishandled and abused. That is all the more reason to read the Bible for ourselves.

In my first year of college I went to a mainline, denominational, liberal arts college. The professor was teaching Intro to the Bible or New Testament. I don't remember which. One day I asked him if he read the Bible and he said, "I'm teaching the Bible." So I restated my question, to which he replied, "I don't get what you are asking me." So I restated the question as, "Has it been years since you actually picked up a Bible and read it?" And he said, "Yes, but I don't see your point." I knew it had to be true, that he didn't read the Bible, in order to believe what he believed and to teach what he was teaching. That man didn't believe or even know the Bible or, for that matter, he probably didn't even know the God of the Bible, even though he was teaching the Bible.

As you begin to listen and hear God, be sure that you spend as much time reading His Word, the Bible, as listening to Him. Test what you hear by what the Bible says. Test what others say God told them by what the Bible says.

MAKING IT PERSONAL

1. Are you reading God's Word on a regular basis? _____
   _____

2. Do you regularly test what you hear being said by others by how it compares to what God's Word has to say?
   _____
   _____

3. If satan used scripture when he tempted Jesus, is it possible for people to use the Bible today and be wrong? How should this impact us? _____
   _____

DAY 5

WEEK 1 | LESSON 5

DAILY LESSON

TIME TO LISTEN

Write in the space below whatever God may be speaking to you. Don't censor it as you write. If a song comes to mind pay attention to the words and write them. If scripture, write down the reference or the verse, if random thoughts write them. If you see images in your mind write them. Afterward ask God for discernment as to what each thing means.

_____

_____

_____

_____

_____

_____

_____

_____

_____

_____

_____

_____

_____

_____

_____

_____

_____

_____

_____

_____

_____

_____

_____

_____

_____

_____

PURPLE	Is used when God is speaking directly in the first person.
GREEN	Is used when a passage is talking about God speaking.
GOLD	Is used when God is speaking through non-verbal communication.
BROWN	Is used when Man is speaking on God's behalf in the Third Person.
BLUE	Is used for Angels speaking on God's behalf or a vision or a dream.
RED	These are the Words of Jesus.

ACTS CHAPTER 6

1 And in those days, when the number of the disciples was multiplied, there arose a murmuring of the Grecians against the Hebrews, because their widows were neglected in the daily ministration.

2 Then the twelve called the multitude of the disciples to them, and said, It is not reason that we should leave the word of God, and serve tables.

3 Why, brothers, look you out among you seven men of honest report, full of the Holy Ghost and wisdom, whom we may appoint over this business.

4 But we will give ourselves continually to prayer, and to the ministry of the word.

5 And the saying pleased the whole multitude: and they chose Stephen, a man full of faith and of the Holy Ghost, and Philip, and Prochorus, and Nicanor, and Timon, and Parmenas, and Nicolas a proselyte of Antioch:

6 Whom they set before the apostles: and when they had prayed, they laid their hands on them.

7 And the word of God increased; and the number of the disciples multiplied in Jerusalem greatly; and a great company of the priests were obedient to the faith.

8 And Stephen, full of faith and power, did great wonders and miracles among the people.

9 Then there arose certain of the synagogue, which is called the synagogue of the Libertines, and Cyrenians, and Alexandrians, and of them of Cilicia and of Asia, disputing with Stephen.

10 And they were not able to resist the wisdom and the spirit by which he spoke.

11 Then they suborned men, which said, We have heard him speak blasphemous words against Moses, and against God.

12 And they stirred up the people, and the elders, and the scribes, and came on him, and caught him, and brought him to the council,

13 And set up false witnesses, which said, This man ceases not to speak blasphemous words against this holy place, and the law:

14 For we have heard him say, that this Jesus of Nazareth shall destroy this place, and shall change the customs which Moses delivered us.

15 And all that sat in the council, looking steadfastly on him, saw his face as it had been the face of an angel.

FIRST DEACON EXPERIENCES GOD'S POWER.

Stephen was the first deacon and God used him to show God's power by miracles. (Acts 6:8)

PERSONAL NOTES

_____

_____

_____

_____

_____

_____

_____

_____

_____

_____

_____

_____

_____

_____

_____

_____

_____

_____

_____

_____

DAY 6

WEEK 1 | LESSON 6

DAILY LESSON

SOME THINGS TO PONDER

1. How would you choose a person today to be a deacon who is full of the Holy Spirit? _____
   _____
   _____

2. How was it obvious that Stephen was full of the Holy Spirit? _____
   _____
   _____

3. Why would the religious leaders react to Stephen when God was doing miracles through Him?
   _____
   _____

4. What do you think happened to Stephen's face at the end of the chapter? Why would this happen?
   _____
   _____

LEARNING TO HEAR GOD - DAY 6 – TIME TO BE STILL

In our frenetic pace of life today, it is a wonder anyone ever hears from God. In many homes the alarm clock goes off and everyone's feet hit the floor running. That is, after too many snoozes. The TV goes on and the iPods come off their docking stations as the earbuds enter the ear canals. We are definitely in a tuned-in world. In our spare minutes we check our email, our Facebook, our tweets and our 5-10 other social media connection points. We make sure our plants are alive in Farmville and our virtual pets have been fed, then we take care of the real pet and our real spouses, kids and other responsibilities.

We hurriedly get into our cars and fight for control of what music we will listen to, drop off anyone we need to drop off, pick up anything we need to pick up, and arrive at work, school or whatever activities we have planned for our day. At the end of our daytime activities we rush to pick up whatever or whoever we need to pick up, prepare or drive to our meal with some form of media blaring in the background before we turn on our favorite shows, while playing a quick game or two, while again checking our eBay account, emails, Facebook and 5-10 other social media connection points before saying hello to our spouse and good night to our plugged-in kids, wondering if they even heard us, only to collapse into bed exhausted.

Sound at all familiar or close to your reality? What was missing? Where is God?

We need—no, it is critical—to be honest, I can't find words to stress how urgent it is that we take time to be still. We HAVE TO hear from God. This is not an option that we can let slide. It is more critical that you hear from God than to catch up on the latest scores, or gossip, your soap opera or your favorite sitcom, or to check the daily stock reports.

David was a king and a warrior. If you want to know busy, try leading an army of soldiers or a nation that is at war. But David took time to listen and God gave him specific directions that made him a great warrior and a great king. One thing you will notice in Acts is that many times God gave people a vision when they were in prayer or a dream when they were sleeping or spoke to them when they were meditating.

Yes, God can speak to us over the roar of a crashing wave, in a concert where you can't hear your own voice or in a vacuum where there is no other sound. God is not limited to speaking in the quiet. It is we who are limited. It is hard to listen to many things at the same time.

Normally the easiest way to learn to hear God is to turn off all the stuff, noise, and distractions and make time to listen. Once you are good at listening, you can better hear God over the noise.

It is more important than anything you have in your schedule. He is more important than anyone in your schedule. You are more important to Him than anyone who demands your time.

I know, mother of a child or more, that you can't imagine where you could squeeze a minute in. I know, business leader trying to keep the business afloat that you feel that you are drowning in demands. I know that as a student having to pay your way through school, you can't find an ounce of strength left for another demand. BUT, this relationship and hearing God will actually lift your burden if you will just do it.

Make some time to be still and start to listen. Do it now!

DAY 6

DAILY LESSON

WEEK 1 | LESSON 6

MAKING IT PERSONAL

1. If someone were to look at your daily calendar what are the things they would see that might be a higher priority than time with God? _____

_____

_____

2. What will it take for you to create time in your schedule to listen to God? _____

_____

_____

TIME TO LISTEN

Write in the space below whatever God may be speaking to you. Don't censor it as you write. If a song comes to mind pay attention to the words and write them. If scripture, write down the reference or the verse, if random thoughts write them. If you see images in your mind write them. Afterward ask God for discernment as to what each thing means.

_____

_____

_____

_____

_____

_____

_____

_____

_____

_____

_____

_____

_____

_____

_____

_____

_____

_____

DAY 7

PURPLE	Is used when God is speaking directly in the first person.
GREEN	Is used when a passage is talking about God speaking.
GOLD	Is used when God is speaking through non-verbal communication.
BROWN	Is used when Man is speaking on God's behalf in the Third Person.
BLUE	Is used for Angels speaking on God's behalf or a vision or a dream.
RED	These are the Words of Jesus.

ACTS CHAPTER 7

1 Then said the high priest, Are these things so?

2 And he said, Men, brothers, and fathers, listen; The God of glory appeared to our father Abraham, when he was in Mesopotamia, before he dwelled in Charran,

3 And said to him, Get you out of your country, and from your kindred, and come into the land which I shall show you.

4 Then came he out of the land of the Chaldaeans, and dwelled in Charran: and from there, when his father was dead, he removed him into this land, wherein you now dwell.

5 And he gave him none inheritance in it, no, not so much as to set his foot on: yet he promised that he would give it to him for a possession, and to his seed after him, when as yet he had no child.

6 And God spoke on this wise, That his seed should sojourn in a strange land; and that they should bring them into bondage, and entreat them evil four hundred years.

7 And the nation to whom they shall be in bondage will I judge, said God: and after that shall they come forth, and serve me in this place.

8 And he gave him the covenant of circumcision: and so Abraham begat Isaac, and circumcised him the eighth day; and Isaac begat Jacob; and Jacob begat the twelve patriarchs.

9 And the patriarchs, moved with envy, sold Joseph into Egypt: but God was with him,

10 And delivered him out of all his afflictions, and gave him favor and wisdom in the sight of Pharaoh king of Egypt; and he made him governor over Egypt and all his house.

11 Now there came a dearth over all the land of Egypt and Chanaan, and great affliction: and our fathers found no sustenance.

12 But when Jacob heard that there was corn in Egypt, he sent out our fathers first.

13 And at the second time Joseph was made known to

ANGELS & JESUS AT DEATH'S DOOR

Stephen was the first martyr of the new church. He was stoned to death for testifying of Jesus. As he was dying he saw angels and he saw Jesus at the right hand of God. Many have testified of seeing angels or Jesus before they pass this life. (Acts 7:55-56)

his brothers; and Joseph's kindred was made known to Pharaoh.

14 Then sent Joseph, and called his father Jacob to him, and all his kindred, three score and fifteen souls.

15 So Jacob went down into Egypt, and died, he, and our fathers,

16 And were carried over into Sychem, and laid in the sepulcher that Abraham bought for a sum of money of the sons of Emmor the father of Sychem.

17 But when the time of the promise drew near, which God had sworn to Abraham, the people grew and multiplied in Egypt,

18 Till another king arose, which knew not Joseph.

19 The same dealt subtly with our kindred, and evil entreated our fathers, so that they cast out their young children, to the end they might not live.

20 In which time Moses was born, and was exceeding fair, and nourished up in his father's house three months:

21 And when he was cast out, Pharaoh's daughter took him up, and nourished him for her own son.

22 And Moses was learned in all the wisdom of the Egyptians, and was mighty in words and in deeds.

23 And when he was full forty years old, it came into his heart to visit his brothers the children of Israel.

24 And seeing one of them suffer wrong, he defended him, and avenged him that was oppressed, and smote the Egyptian:

25 For he supposed his brothers would have understood

how that God by his hand would deliver them: but they understood not.

26 And the next day he showed himself to them as they strove, and would have set them at one again, saying, Sirs, you are brothers; why do you wrong one to another?

27 But he that did his neighbor wrong thrust him away, saying, Who made you a ruler and a judge over us?

28 Will you kill me, as you did the Egyptian yesterday?

29 Then fled Moses at this saying, and was a stranger in the land of Madian, where he begat two sons.

30 And when forty years were expired, there appeared to him in the wilderness of mount Sina an angel of the Lord in a flame of fire in a bush.

31 When Moses saw it, he wondered at the sight: and as he drew near to behold it, the voice of the LORD came to him,

32 Saying, I am the God of your fathers, the God of Abraham, and the God of Isaac, and the God of Jacob. Then Moses trembled, and dared not behold.

33 Then said the Lord to him, Put off your shoes from your feet: for the place where you stand is holy ground.

34 I have seen, I have seen the affliction of my people which is in Egypt, and I have heard their groaning, and am come down to deliver them. And now come, I will send you into Egypt.

35 This Moses whom they refused, saying, Who made you a ruler and a judge? the same did God send to be a ruler and a deliverer by the hand of the angel which appeared to him in the bush.

36 He brought them out, after that he had showed wonders and signs in the land of Egypt, and in the Red sea, and in the wilderness forty years.

37 This is that Moses, which said to the children of Israel, A prophet shall the Lord your God raise up to you of your brothers, like to me; him shall you hear.

38 This is he, that was in the church in the wilderness with the angel which spoke to him in the mount Sina, and with our fathers: who received the lively oracles to give to us:

39 To whom our fathers would not obey, but thrust him from them, and in their hearts turned back again into Egypt,

40 Saying to Aaron, Make us gods to go before us: for as for this Moses, which brought us out of the land of Egypt, we know not what is become of him.

41 And they made a calf in those days, and offered sacrifice to the idol, and rejoiced in the works of their own hands.

42 Then God turned, and gave them up to worship the host of heaven; as it is written in the book of the prophets, O you house of Israel, have you offered to me slain beasts and sacrifices by the space of forty years in the wilderness?

43 Yes, you took up the tabernacle of Moloch, and the star of your god Remphan, figures which you made to worship them: and I will carry you away beyond Babylon.

44 Our fathers had the tabernacle of witness in the wilderness, as he had appointed, speaking to Moses, that he should make it according to the fashion that he had seen.

45 Which also our fathers that came after brought in with Jesus into the possession of the Gentiles, whom God drove out before the face of our fathers, to the days of David;

46 Who found favor before God, and desired to find a tabernacle for the God of Jacob.

47 But Solomon built him an house.

48 However, the most High dwells not in temples made with hands; as said the prophet,

49 Heaven is my throne, and earth is my footstool: what house will you build me? said the Lord: or what is the place of my rest?

50 Has not my hand made all these things?

51 You stiffnecked and uncircumcised in heart and ears, you do always resist the Holy Ghost: as your fathers did, so do you.

52 Which of the prophets have not your fathers persecuted? and they have slain them which showed before of the coming of the Just One; of whom you have been now the betrayers and murderers:

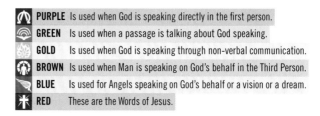

	PURPLE	Is used when God is speaking directly in the first person.
	GREEN	Is used when a passage is talking about God speaking.
	GOLD	Is used when God is speaking through non-verbal communication.
	BROWN	Is used when Man is speaking on God's behalf in the Third Person.
	BLUE	Is used for Angels speaking on God's behalf or a vision or a dream.
	RED	These are the Words of Jesus.

53 Who have received the law by the disposition of angels, and have not kept it.

54 When they heard these things, they were cut to the heart, and they gnashed on him with their teeth.

55 But he, being full of the Holy Ghost, looked up steadfastly into heaven, and saw the glory of God, and Jesus standing on the right hand of God,

56 And said, Behold, I see the heavens opened, and the Son of man standing on the right hand of God.

57 Then they cried out with a loud voice, and stopped their ears, and ran on him with one accord,

58 And cast him out of the city, and stoned him: and the witnesses laid down their clothes at a young man's feet, whose name was Saul.

59 And they stoned Stephen, calling on God, and saying, Lord Jesus, receive my spirit.

60 And he kneeled down, and cried with a loud voice, Lord, lay not this sin to their charge. And when he had said this, he fell asleep.

PERSONAL NOTES

_____
_____
_____
_____
_____
_____
_____
_____
_____
_____
_____
_____
_____
_____
_____
_____
_____
_____
_____
_____
_____
_____
_____
_____
_____
_____
_____
_____
_____
_____
_____
_____
_____
_____

DAY 7

DAILY LESSON

WEEK 1 | LESSON 7

SOME THINGS TO PONDER

1. Look at Stephen's use of Old Testament Scripture throughout his sermon. Why would this be important in light of who he was preaching to? _____
_____
_____

2. What was Stephen seeing and experiencing while those around him were filled with rage and anger and thoughts of murder? _____
_____
_____

3. Stephen saw Jesus and God the Father; who else can you think of who saw God the Father? (*Answer below*)
_____
_____

4. Have you ever seen a vision? How often? Do you believe you can see one? _____
_____

Answer: Adam and Eve, Moses on mount Sanai, etc.

LEARNING TO HEAR GOD - DAY 7 - IS THIS ME OR IS IT GOD, IS IT ME OR IS IT GOD.....?

Many people get stuck while listening to God's voice as they listen, asking themselves the question, "Is this me imagining things or is it God's voice?" In my experience that is an almost universal question. It is the exception to find the person who can confidently say, "I've always known God's voice since I was a kid." I know people who have. We have to watch out for arrogance and believing that we are always right and that it is not possible for our own imagination to ever affect what we hear.

How do we know if it is me or if it is God? Well there are those times when God shows up in human form or there is a voice from heaven. Those are awesome when they happen but that is not the normal way that God speaks. You will be learning much about how God speaks and how to listen but I want to encourage you as you listen and write down what you believe the Lord may be speaking to you, don't censor it.

DAILY LESSON

We will never write anything down if our censor meter is too high. Don't hear me say that everything that comes to your mind or spirit is from God. I'm saying while you're writing it down, don't censor it, and then examine it and see if it is God.

- Do you believe God can speak?
- Are you open to the idea that He can speak to you?
- Do you believe that scripture shows us a God who likes to communicate with people?
- Do you believe that God wants to and will talk to you?

The difference in those two lines of questions is in one case you believe God can, in another you believe that he wants to and will, do something. Those are two different levels of belief. Many believe God can do anything, but that He doesn't or won't for a myriad of reasons.

It took me a long time to get past questioning whether the things God was speaking to me were God or my own imagination. I teach on day 20 about how it is possible to operate in our own imagination. That is a real issue. The false prophets were listening to and prophesying what their own imaginations came up with. They said what people wanted to hear and said they had a Word from the Lord, but were just operating in their own imagination.

For now, please don't worry about that. Trust God to speak to you and listen. Don't censor. We will learn to discern the difference between the different voices that can interfere and the voice of God. Doing this will help you immeasurably. Many people get stuck wanting to make sure they have it perfect and can never write anything down that the Lord might be speaking because of fear they might get it wrong.

Chill out. You will likely get it wrong one day. We don't practice stoning people if they aren't 100% right. I've often wondered what a school of prophets that is spoken of several times in the Old Testament was like. Were prophets being trained? Did they always get it right in class all the time? Or, did they go through training to learn to discern with accuracy what came from the Lord and what didn't—I don't know, we are told very little about what those schools were like.

Imagine you are in the school of learning to hear God. It is okay to get a B. You will learn how to get A's, and if you get a B or a C you can still graduate and know your Father's voice.

DAY 7

DAILY LESSON

WEEK 1 | LESSON 7

MAKING IT PERSONAL

1. Have you struggled with that nagging question regarding whether you are making something up or whether it is truly God speaking to you? _____

   _____

   _____

2. Do you believe that God can speak today? Will speak? Will speak to YOU? _____

   _____

   _____

3. Have you written anything down during the listening time? Can you tell if any of it was definitely God? Is there anything that you think might have not been God but rather a wandering mind or your imagination?

   _____

   _____

   _____

TIME TO LISTEN

Write in the space below whatever God may be speaking to you. Don't censor it as you write. If a song comes to mind pay attention to the words and write them. If scripture, write down the reference or the verse, if random thoughts write them. If you see images in your mind write them. Afterward ask God for discernment as to what each thing means.

_____

_____

_____

_____

_____

_____

_____

_____

_____

_____

_____

_____

GOD SPEAKS

LEARN HOW TO HEAR GOD

A JOURNEY THROUGH THE BOOK OF ACTS

SECTION

2

WEEK 2 | LESSONS 8-14
STUDY GUIDE

WEEK 2 | LESSONS 8-14

HOW TO LISTEN WELL – YOU CAN'T TELL WHAT GOD'S SAYING IF YOU DON'T LISTEN

It is an age-old problem. Wives know it all too well. We've all experienced it many times. Parents experience it with their kids. Kids know what it feels like from interacting with their parents. Bosses experience it, employees experience it and maybe pastors can relate most of all. It's expressed something like this, "They are hearing me speak but they aren't really listening!" Can you relate? Isn't it frustrating? How do you think God feels? He is speaking to His sheep but they aren't listening. Most of us have never been taught how. Don't blame your pastor or denomination. It is right there in scripture for all of us to discover. Don't worry, we can discover it together.

I have spent 14 years learning how to hear God's voice. And 10 years ago a pastor asked me to come and teach his people how to hear God. At the time I wasn't ready to explain how to someone else. I was still learning to hear God myself. His request motivated me and recently God called me and compelled me to complete this task.

A CRAZY PRAYER

It all began with a crazy prayer of a Baptist youth pastor, me. I was torn while making a decision where both options were good. The long version of this story is in my book, The Jesus Training Manual, but it bears repeating. The decision that I faced was whether to stay at the church where I had been on staff for 5 years and loved. Or, should I pursue what I went to college and seminary to study and had committed my life to which was church planting overseas. Both answers involved serving God and both were great opportunities. Church planting was a much more difficult road but I had already processed the cost of leaving the US, raising funds, and learning a language and was willing to pay the cost.

Several people had told me God was telling them that I was supposed to stay. At the time, I had a hard time accepting that because of what I had been taught about God speaking. These were a dear friend and the lead pastor at our church. They had a vested interest in me staying. I was torn because

if I stayed I would always wonder whether I had taken the easy road. So, if God wanted me to stay I wanted it to be supernatural. If God answered this prayer there would be no looking back.

I gave the Lord two options. I know that sounds presumptuous and crazy but the Lord knew I would do whatever He wanted; I just needed it to be clear. I don't know why I picked the two options that I did but I asked the Lord that if He wanted me to stay to either drop a granite stone out of the sky or send someone to walk up off the street and tell me God told me to stay. Either of those and I would stay. Then I fasted for 4 days and committed to going overseas unless God intervened. Well, just 4 days after my fast the Lord did intervene in an amazing and bizarre way.

A guy with long, hair and a long beard showed up at the church and asked for a pastor. I was the only one around at that time though we had 10 pastors on staff. This man told me with tears in his eyes and a trembling voice that He had been sent there by God with a message. He said, "Sometimes we feel like God wants us to go far away like another country and that is where He can use us, when in reality He wants us to stay right where we are and that is where He is going to use us to make a difference." Wow! I was stunned. How could this happen? How did this guy know? He went on to tell me two other things that I had been praying about, sang me a song, kissed me on the cheek, laughing, and left the building.

As I processed this with my wife and close friends, I had to conclude that this man had heard from God. To attribute this to the devil would give the devil more power than my God and make him more personal and able to answer my prayers. God had done this. Here I was with theological degrees and 12 years of church ministry under my belt and I couldn't say that I had heard God except maybe a few times. I wanted to hear God like this man did. That was what I wanted to learn more than anything.

BODY, SOUL AND SPIRIT

In 1 Thessalonians 5:23 Paul writes, "And the God of peace himself sanctify you wholly; and may your spirit and soul and body be preserved entire, without blame at the coming of our Lord Jesus Christ." (AKJV). Here we see that God is at work in all three parts of our being. Scripture has much to say about our spirit and our soul. It is amazing if you study what the Bible says about our human spirit. Our human spirit is spoken of more than the Holy Spirit or evil spirits, though most people have never heard any teaching on our human spirit. If you don't believe that scripture says more about our human spirit then I challenge you to examine every passage related to the Hebrew and Greek word spirit. Then for each verse put it into one of three categories, The Holy Spirit, evil spirits or human spirit. What you will find will amaze you.

Why does the Bible talk so much about our human spirit but we know so little? Unfortunately, I don't know the answer to that question. It is true of many subjects that the Bible takes very seriously and are vital to our Christian walk. I truly believe that the enemy would love for you to be ignorant about your human spirit and about hearing God's voice.

For a more extended treatment of the subject of our human spirit, please visit, www.operationlightforce. com, and I would encourage you to go deeper with that subject.

God is spirit and that part of our being is the part which is most like God. When God created us in His image, many believe that it is our spirit that He put within us, separate from the Holy Spirit that is most like Him. Everyone has a spirit. Unbelievers have a spirit but that spirit is not fully alive apart from a relationship with God.

God is spirit and He speaks most often Spirit to spirit. The problem is that most of us are unaware of our spirit and, for that matter, that we even have a spirit. In the west we pay most of our attention to our bodies. Some pay attention to their souls. Psychology is the science of the soul and comes from the Greek word for soul. Our spirit and soul are the eternal part of our being.

If God is spirit and we are spirit then God speaks spirit to spirit. Scripture says it so many different ways. Jesus said in John 4:23-24 "But the hour comes, and now is, when the true worshippers shall worship the Father in spirit and in truth: for the Father seeks such to worship him. 24 God is a Spirit: and they that worship him must worship him in spirit and in truth." Our spirits are to be engaged in worship of the Lord. In the same way when God communicates with us we first discern what God is saying to us in our spirit. My friends from Ghana West Africa say I know it in my knower (sounds like I know it in my Noah). There are is describing their spirit communing with God.

A STILL SMALL VOICE

In 1 Kings 19:12 we read, "And after the earthquake a fire; but the LORD was not in the fire: and after the fire a still small voice." Elijah had become discouraged by the threats of Jezebel to take his life and was feeling all alone. The Lord sent an angel to feed him, gave Elijah rest and then communed with Elijah. He told Elijah to stand inside a cave. Then a mighty wind came by, but the Lord was not in the wind. Then an earthquake shook the ground but God was not in the quake. Then fire came but God was not in the fire. Finally a still small voice came and God spoke in a still small voice. Many people have described it like this. A small voice within.

For me, God didn't sound like I expected Him to, all I experienced were images in my mind and thoughts running through my head. How distracting. Could God speak up so I could hear Him over the thoughts and images in my mind? As I learned to hear God's voice, I realized that God had been speaking to me all along. The images I found so distracting were actually visions from God. The thoughts were God speaking to my spirit and my mind interpreting His message.

If you hear someone speaking, your mind is processing her words as well as her expressions, inflections and body language. All of that combined give you the context to know what she is saying. Without knowing it we are repeating in our minds the things they are saying to us. In the same way God speaks to our spirit and our mind replays what God is saying.

VISIONS

It is also vital as you listen to God to pay attention to images that come into your mind. I had always thought of these as distractions but I have learned that many times God is speaking through vision in the images within my head. Write down what you see in your head. Recently I was with a group of teenagers and a young girl saw herself walking on the beach. A man came up to her and told her not to be afraid, He was her Father from heaven and He loved her, she was beautiful and not to let anyone tell her otherwise. Likewise, through no prompting other than to pay attention to images they saw, over half the group saw images or scenes.

If you have not noticed already, you will see before this study is finished that there are a good number of visions recorded throughout the book of Acts. Now remember that Acts is following just a couple of the apostles' lives. Imagine this multiplied in the lives of the 120 in the upper room—each of them having visions and unbelievers having visions coming to them as well. There were thousands added to the church on a regular basis. Not every vision that God gave was recorded, only those that were part of the stories they chose to record.

Visions are a normal part of how God communicates with us, His people. So are dreams and, in scripture, so are angels. Many angelic encounters were in dreams or visions. Some had physical manifestations as well. God's Word is full of these kinds of examples, and God has not given the angels an extended vacation since the church was born, nor has He stopped speaking through dreams and visions.

Take the time to listen to God and make it a focused commitment to be in His presence. Write down the thoughts that come to your mind and the images you see. If you have a dream, write it down. Ask God what the meaning is behind what He is saying to you.

HIS FIRST WORDS TO ME

When I first started listening God said only one thing clearly to me. Trust Me. In my life He was saying trust Me with your finances, your future, your career, and trust Me to teach you. That trusting led to 3 years where I spent every day in the scriptures for hours, and neither my wife nor I had a job, position or title. He did provide for every single bill. I didn't have a ministry, didn't raise funds, and didn't have royalties from books. All the provision was miraculous. We know that we still live that way, though God has blessed us in some specific ways over the years.

The next thing God clearly said to me was, "Can you just be with me?" I wanted the 3- and 5- year plans and goals. I wanted to know what He wanted me to "DO." I had degrees and talents but God knew that I wasn't ready to do anything for Him. It made no sense to me and it was hard to believe this was God speaking to me. What if the devil was just trying to keep me from doing what I was supposed to be doing, or what if all this time in God's Word was me being lazy? But as I listened He was clearly saying, "Just be with me."

Now when I listen I get pages of material for people that I minister to. I've been with God and realize that powerful ministry flows out of being with Him, and I am content to be with Him and obey Him, no matter what the cost.

DON'T BE SURPRISED

Don't set yourself up with expectations. Just listen. If God doesn't say much but focuses on one issue in your life, don't be surprised. Obey Him, if you want to keep hearing. What if I had just taken a job, because I had some incredible offers? I doubt that I would be writing this. I would have been too busy in ministry to spend the quantity of time that I was able to spend with the Lord. I don't expect God to give as radical of a call to you, but He might. I have no regrets, and as aresult of that season my life and ministry have been transformed. If God does challenge you as deeply as He did me, I rejoice with you in the wonderful things that will become of this journey.

Don't be afraid, just make the time and take the time to listen. Obey Him. Allow God to deal with any areas He chooses to.

Most people need to find a quiet time and a quiet place. Moms, I know for many of you that sounds impossible. I pray you find creative ways and times to make that time. It will empower you in your mothering and as a spouse.

DAY 8

WEEK 2 | LESSON 8

PURPLE	Is used when God is speaking directly in the first person.
GREEN	Is used when a passage is talking about God speaking.
GOLD	Is used when God is speaking through non-verbal communication.
BROWN	Is used when Man is speaking on God's behalf in the Third Person.
BLUE	Is used for Angels speaking on God's behalf or a vision or a dream.
RED	These are the Words of Jesus.

ACTS CHAPTER 8

1 And Saul was consenting to his death. And at that time there was a great persecution against the church which was at Jerusalem; and they were all scattered abroad throughout the regions of Judaea and Samaria, except the apostles.

2 And devout men carried Stephen to his burial, and made great lamentation over him.

3 As for Saul, he made havoc of the church, entering into every house, and haling men and women committed them to prison.

4 Therefore they that were scattered abroad went everywhere where preaching the word.

5 Then Philip went down to the city of Samaria, and preached Christ to them.

6 And the people with one accord gave heed to those things which Philip spoke, hearing and seeing the miracles which he did.

7 For unclean spirits, crying with loud voice, came out of many that were possessed with them: and many taken with palsies, and that were lame, were healed.

8 And there was great joy in that city.

9 But there was a certain man, called Simon, which beforetime in the same city used sorcery, and bewitched the people of Samaria, giving out that himself was some great one:

10 To whom they all gave heed, from the least to the greatest, saying, This man is the great power of God.

11 And to him they had regard, because that of long time he had bewitched them with sorceries.

12 But when they believed Philip preaching the things concerning the kingdom of God, and the name of Jesus Christ, they were baptized, both men and women.

13 Then Simon himself believed also: and when he was baptized, he continued with Philip, and wondered, beholding the miracles and signs which were done.

14 Now when the apostles which were at Jerusalem heard that Samaria had received the word of God, they sent to them Peter and John:

ANGEL GIVES DIRECTION
The Angel of the Lord told Philip where to go and how to get there but didn't give him details. The key for Philip was getting clear directions from the Lord. His response was to obey and not to ask questions. Then God spoke by the Holy Spirit to Philip, giving detailed directions to get into the chariot. Again, Philip simply obeyed the voice of God.

15 Who, when they were come down, prayed for them, that they might receive the Holy Ghost:

16 (For as yet he was fallen on none of them: only they were baptized in the name of the Lord Jesus.)

17 Then laid they their hands on them, and they received the Holy Ghost.

18 And when Simon saw that through laying on of the apostles' hands the Holy Ghost was given, he offered them money,

19 Saying, Give me also this power, that on whomsoever I lay hands, he may receive the Holy Ghost.

20 But Peter said to him, Your money perish with you, because you have thought that the gift of God may be purchased with money.

21 You have neither part nor lot in this matter: for your heart is not right in the sight of God.

22 Repent therefore of this your wickedness, and pray God, if perhaps the thought of your heart may be forgiven you.

23 For I perceive that you are in the gall of bitterness, and in the bond of iniquity.

24 Then answered Simon, and said, Pray you to the LORD for me, that none of these things which you have spoken come on me.

25 And they, when they had testified and preached the word of the Lord, returned to Jerusalem, and preached the gospel in many villages of the Samaritans.

DAY 8

PURPLE	Is used when God is speaking directly in the first person.
GREEN	Is used when a passage is talking about God speaking.
GOLD	Is used when God is speaking through non-verbal communication.
BROWN	Is used when Man is speaking on God's behalf in the Third Person.
BLUE	Is used for Angels speaking on God's behalf or a vision or a dream.
RED	These are the Words of Jesus.

26 And the angel of the Lord spoke to Philip, saying, Arise, and go toward the south to the way that goes down from Jerusalem to Gaza, which is desert.

27 And he arose and went: and, behold, a man of Ethiopia, an eunuch of great authority under Candace queen of the Ethiopians, who had the charge of all her treasure, and had come to Jerusalem for to worship,

28 Was returning, and sitting in his chariot read Esaias the prophet.

29 Then the Spirit said to Philip, Go near, and join yourself to this chariot.

30 And Philip ran thither to him, and heard him read the prophet Esaias, and said, Understand you what you read?

31 And he said, How can I, except some man should guide me? And he desired Philip that he would come up and sit with him.

32 The place of the scripture which he read was this, He was led as a sheep to the slaughter; and like a lamb dumb before his shearer, so opened he not his mouth:

33 In his humiliation his judgment was taken away: and who shall declare his generation? for his life is taken from the earth.

34 And the eunuch answered Philip, and said, I pray you, of whom speaks the prophet this? of himself, or of some other man?

35 Then Philip opened his mouth, and began at the same scripture, and preached to him Jesus.

36 And as they went on their way, they came to a certain water: and the eunuch said, See, here is water; what does hinder me to be baptized?

37 And Philip said, If you believe with all your heart, you may. And he answered and said, I believe that Jesus Christ is the Son of God.

38 And he commanded the chariot to stand still: and they went down both into the water, both Philip and the eunuch; and he baptized him.

39 And when they were come up out of the water, the Spirit of the Lord caught away Philip, that the eunuch saw him no more: and he went on his way rejoicing.

40 But Philip was found at Azotus: and passing through he preached in all the cities, till he came to Caesarea.

GOD SPEAKS DIRECTLY BY THE SPIRIT OF GOD

a. The Holy Ghost bears witness to the truth (Acts 5:32)

b. The Spirit spoke to Philip and told him to get in the chariot of the Ethiopian (Acts 8:29)

c. The Spirit spoke to Peter about his vision (Acts 10:19-20)

d. The Spirit told the church to separate Paul and Barnabas unto the Lord (Acts 13:2)

e. Paul and Barnabas were told by the Holy Spirit not to go to Asia or to Bithynia (Acts 16:6-7)

f. Paul was compelled by the Spirit to go to Jerusalem (Acts 20:22)

g. The Holy Spirit was speaking everywhere Paul went telling Paul that he would be jailed and afflicted when he went to Jerusalem (Acts 20:23)

PERSONAL NOTES

_____
_____
_____
_____
_____
_____
_____
_____
_____
_____
_____
_____
_____
_____
_____

DAY 8

DAILY LESSON

WEEK 2 | LESSON 8

SOME THINGS TO PONDER

1. What was happening when this deacon named Philip was preaching that got the people excited and caused many to believe? _____

_____

_____

2. What message did the angel bring to Philip? Have you ever encountered an angel? _____

_____

_____

3. What message did the Holy Spirit speak to Philip? How do you think that Philip hearing this message was different from what you are doing as you listen daily? _____

_____

_____

4. What source did Philip refer to as he taught the Ethiopian man? _____

_____

_____

LEARNING TO HEAR GOD - DAY 8 – YOU HAVE A SPIRIT

I cannot believe how little we have been taught about our human spirit. The Bible talks so much about our human spirit, but I have only heard two people ever teach on it. Earlier we observed that the Bible talks more about our human spirits than it does about The Holy Spirit or evil spirits.

You see, we are created in God's image and God is Spirit. God relates to us Spirit to spirit. For many of you, what I am saying right now is totally foreign and you find it hard to believe or grasp.

In the west, especially, we are so aware of our physical bodies. It seems like every commercial is about how this product or that product will give you the perfect body so everyone can see your body, so you can feel great in your body. Okay, you get my point. Next we are aware to varying degrees with our psyche, or soul. Our soul, we are told, is our mind, will, and emotions. Most guys are less aware of their emotions than women are, but we all live much of our lives either in our mind, will, and emotions.

The most eternal and God-like part of our being is our spirit, and yet there is so little teaching on our human spirit. That is not because the Bible is silent on the subject, but because we have ignored it.

The reason this is important is that God often communicates with our spirit, and for us to get good at hearing God speaking we must become more aware of our human spirit. On our website, www.operationlightforce.com, there is biblical teaching on the human spirit as well as a complete list of scriptural references on the subject that will help you understand this subject better.

But here's the thing: the place where most people begin to have an awareness of God speaking to them is in their mind. Sometimes in the Bible, God or angels would show up in person, but more often God would speak in a still small voice, which is, in reality, His Spirit speaking to our spirit and our mind processing what came in through our spirit.

For many people, when they begin to hear God it seems like their own thoughts. Most people go through a debate in their minds as they begin to hear God that goes something like this, "Is this me making this up or is this God?" To be honest, I struggled with that for a long time and, as much as I have learned about hearing God, sometimes I still do.

While people are learning to hear God and journaling what they believe God is speaking to them, I encourage them not to censor what they write down. For some, they will be writing down the things they are thinking about, asking God for, or something else that their mind engages in, and it isn't God speaking to them. Some people spend their entire time talking to God and don't take time to listen. Others are tormented by demonic voices and visions and struggle to hear God over those voices. Most people, when they take the time and ask God to speak to them, will begin to hear that still small voice.

What God speaks to your spirit will begin to play in your mind and may seem like our thoughts, but we are hearing the Father's voice. Keep listening, and become familiar with His voice.

DAY 8

DAILY LESSON

MAKING IT PERSONAL

1. How aware are you of your spirit? Have you ever received teaching about your spirit? _____
   _____
   _____

2. Do you ever use or hear people use expressions like, "My spirit is troubling me," or "Let's play with spirit," or "It feels right in my spirit"? What do you mean or what do you think others mean? _____
   _____
   _____

3. Why do you think that there would be so much in the Bible about our human spirit but so little teaching or understanding about it? What should you do about that? _____
   _____

TIME TO LISTEN

Write in the space below whatever God may be speaking to you. Don't censor it as you write. If a song comes to mind pay attention to the words and write them. If scripture, write down the reference or the verse, if random thoughts write them. If you see images in your mind write them. Afterward ask God for discernment as to what each thing means.

_____

_____

_____

_____

_____

_____

_____

_____

_____

_____

_____

_____

_____

_____

DAY 9

PURPLE	Is used when God is speaking directly in the first person.
GREEN	Is used when a passage is talking about God speaking.
GOLD	Is used when God is speaking through non-verbal communication.
BROWN	Is used when Man is speaking on God's behalf in the Third Person.
BLUE	Is used for Angels speaking on God's behalf or a vision or a dream.
RED	These are the Words of Jesus.

ACTS CHAPTER 9

1 And Saul, yet breathing out threatenings and slaughter against the disciples of the Lord, went to the high priest,

2 And desired of him letters to Damascus to the synagogues, that if he found any of this way, whether they were men or women, he might bring them bound to Jerusalem.

3 And as he journeyed, he came near Damascus: and suddenly there shined round about him a light from heaven:

4 And he fell to the earth, and heard a voice saying to him, Saul, Saul, why persecute you me?

5 And he said, Who are you, Lord? And the Lord said, I am Jesus whom you persecute: it is hard for you to kick against the pricks.

6 And he trembling and astonished said, Lord, what will you have me to do? And the Lord said to him, Arise, and go into the city, and it shall be told you what you must do.

7 And the men which journeyed with him stood speechless, hearing a voice, but seeing no man.

8 And Saul arose from the earth; and when his eyes were opened, he saw no man: but they led him by the hand, and brought him into Damascus.

9 And he was three days without sight, and neither did eat nor drink.

10 And there was a certain disciple at Damascus, named Ananias; and to him said the Lord in a vision, Ananias. And he said, Behold, I am here, Lord.

11 And the Lord said to him, Arise, and go into the street which is called Straight, and inquire in the house of Judas for one called Saul, of Tarsus: for, behold, he prays,

12 And has seen in a vision a man named Ananias coming in, and putting his hand on him, that he might receive his sight.

13 Then Ananias answered, Lord, I have heard by many of this man, how much evil he has done to your saints at Jerusalem:

POST RESURRECTION VISITATION BY JESUS

Jesus came to Saul in a dramatic way. It seems to be more than a vision. We realize it is Jesus when he answers Paul, "I am Jesus." He came in the light of His glory and Paul was blinded. What a dramatic call this was. Nothing says that we cannot encounter Jesus today as Paul did in Acts, and as John did in Revelation.

14 And here he has authority from the chief priests to bind all that call on your name.

15 But the Lord said to him, Go your way: for he is a chosen vessel to me, to bear my name before the Gentiles, and kings, and the children of Israel:

16 For I will show him how great things he must suffer for my name's sake.

17 And Ananias went his way, and entered into the house; and putting his hands on him said, Brother Saul, the Lord, even Jesus, that appeared to you in the way as you came, has sent me, that you might receive your sight, and be filled with the Holy Ghost.

18 And immediately there fell from his eyes as it had been scales: and he received sight immediately, and arose, and was baptized.

19 And when he had received meat, he was strengthened. Then was Saul certain days with the disciples which were at Damascus.

20 And straightway he preached Christ in the synagogues, that he is the Son of God.

21 But all that heard him were amazed, and said; Is not this he that destroyed them which called on this name in Jerusalem, and came here for that intent, that he might bring them bound to the chief priests?

22 But Saul increased the more in strength, and confounded the Jews which dwelled at Damascus, proving that this is very Christ.

23 And after that many days were fulfilled, the Jews took counsel to kill him:

⟁	**PURPLE**	Is used when God is speaking directly in the first person.
⟁	**GREEN**	Is used when a passage is talking about God speaking.
⟁	**GOLD**	Is used when God is speaking through non-verbal communication.
⟁	**BROWN**	Is used when Man is speaking on God's behalf in the Third Person.
⟁	**BLUE**	Is used for Angels speaking on God's behalf or a vision or a dream.
✳	**RED**	These are the Words of Jesus.

24 But their laying await was known of Saul. And they watched the gates day and night to kill him.

25 Then the disciples took him by night, and let him down by the wall in a basket.

26 And when Saul was come to Jerusalem, he assayed to join himself to the disciples: but they were all afraid of him, and believed not that he was a disciple.

27 But Barnabas took him, and brought him to the apostles, and declared to them how he had seen the Lord in the way, and that he had spoken to him, and how he had preached boldly at Damascus in the name of Jesus.

28 And he was with them coming in and going out at Jerusalem.

29 And he spoke boldly in the name of the Lord Jesus, and disputed against the Grecians: but they went about to slay him.

30 Which when the brothers knew, they brought him down to Caesarea, and sent him forth to Tarsus.

31 Then had the churches rest throughout all Judaea and Galilee and Samaria, and were edified; and walking in the fear of the Lord, and in the comfort of the Holy Ghost, were multiplied.

32 And it came to pass, as Peter passed throughout all quarters, he came down also to the saints which dwelled at Lydda.

33 And there he found a certain man named Aeneas, which had kept his bed eight years, and was sick of the palsy.

34 And Peter said to him, Aeneas, Jesus Christ makes you whole: arise, and make your bed. And he arose immediately.

35 And all that dwelled at Lydda and Saron saw him, and turned to the Lord.

36 Now there was at Joppa a certain disciple named Tabitha, which by interpretation is called Dorcas: this woman was full of good works and giving of alms which she did.

37 And it came to pass in those days, that she was

MEN PREACHING GOD'S WORD

a. Peter's sermon was inspired by the Holy Spirit (Acts 2)

b. Stephen preached under the inspiration of the Holy Spirit (Acts 6)

c. Paul preached (Acts 9:27)

d. Saul and Barnabas preached in Salamis (Acts 13:5)

e. Paul preached in Jerusalem (Acts 13:44-49)

f. Paul and Barnabas preached in Antioch (Acts 15:35)

g. Paul and Silas preached to the Jailer and his family (Acts 16:32)

h. Paul and Silas preached in Berea (Acts 17:11-13)

i. Paul preached in Corinth (Acts 18:11)

j. Paul preached the entire counsel of God in Ephesus (Acts 20:27)

sick, and died: whom when they had washed, they laid her in an upper chamber.

38 And for as much as Lydda was near to Joppa, and the disciples had heard that Peter was there, they sent to him two men, desiring him that he would not delay to come to them.

39 Then Peter arose and went with them. When he was come, they brought him into the upper chamber: and all the widows stood by him weeping, and showing the coats and garments which Dorcas made, while she was with them.

40 But Peter put them all forth, and kneeled down, and prayed; and turning him to the body said, Tabitha, arise. And she opened her eyes: and when she saw Peter, she sat up.

41 And he gave her his hand, and lifted her up, and when he had called the saints and widows, presented her alive.

42 And it was known throughout all Joppa; and many believed in the Lord.

43 And it came to pass, that he tarried many days in Joppa with one Simon a tanner.

SOME THINGS TO PONDER

1. In Chapter 9 we have two appearances of Jesus to two different people. What are the similarities in these experiences? _____
_____
_____

2. What are the differences? _____
_____
_____

3. If someone came to you and described an experience like this to you today, would you struggle to believe him? Why? _____
_____
_____

4. Have you ever had a vision where Jesus was in the vision? _____
_____

LEARNING TO HEAR GOD - DAY 9 – I CAN'T GET THESE PICTURES OUT OF MY HEAD.

There can be many things that distract us while we are listening to God's voice. If the baby is in the other room crying, it's hard to listen. If someone is talking and we can hear what she is talking about, it makes it difficult to concentrate. If we are consumed with our own worries and fears, we can struggle to focus on anything else. The list goes on and on, and it takes work to eliminate as many distractions as possible.

The one distraction that I used to battle with was all the pictures in my head. I would get still and try to listen, ask God to speak, and I would have all these thoughts going through my head and all kinds of images, picture and scenes that I would see. Still thinking that God sounded like James Earl Jones and that His voice had to be accompanied by thunder, for years I thought God didn't speak to me. I was waiting for Nirvana, that perfect nothingness, and then I would hear God or have a visitation of some kind.

All the while God was speaking to me. *What? No way! I know I would have heard God if He was speaking to me.* Well, over time I began to realize that those images in my mind were visions. I almost wrote, "Duh, of course they were visions." It seems so obvious now but no one ever taught me to pay attention to the images. Now I write down the images, even if they make no sense.

The first time I was aware that I saw visions was dramatic. They were three-dimensional and I was on the floor of my living room with my wife wondering if I was still breathing. Don't expect it to be that dramatic most of the time. As I began to pay attention to the pictures in my head I began to get an understanding of the images and learned to listen to what God was saying through them.

Again, let me say that not everyone gets visions. But I've observed that a high percentage of people do have visions. When I teach people in conferences about hearing God's voice I often survey after a time of listening and ask, "How many people saw images?" It is normally over 50%.

One time while ministering to a woman, we took a few minutes to listen to God's Spirit. The first thing I saw was a bean fall to the ground. A root popped out of the bean, went into the ground, and then a beanstalk grew up. I wrote down the image but didn't understand the meaning and frankly, I felt a little odd and embarrassed to share it. As the woman who had come for ministry began to share what she had heard, she felt embarrassed to share about seeing a beanstalk grow up and she didn't understand what it meant. I turned my notes toward her so that she could see what I had written. She began to cry, because she knew God had spoken to her. This happens with us very often in ministry. It is normal for us to have two people hear the same thing or totally complementary things. The reason is because it is one Spirit that we are listening to.

As you listen to God today, ask God to give you a vision, and write down any images that come to your mind. Don't worry or stress if nothing comes to your mind. If you do get images or scenes or what seems like a video, write it in as much detail as possible. Then ask God what He is saying through the vision.

DAY 9

DAILY LESSON

MAKING IT PERSONAL

1. Have you ever had pictures in your head while you were praying that you couldn't get rid of?
_____

2. Have you ever had a vision before? _____
_____
_____

3. If you have had a vision, write one down that stands out to you. _____
_____
_____

TIME TO LISTEN

Write in the space below whatever God may be speaking to you. Don't censor it as you write. If a song comes to mind pay attention to the words and write them. If scripture, write down the reference or the verse, if random thoughts write them. If you see images in your mind write them. Afterward ask God for discernment as to what each thing means.

_____
_____
_____
_____
_____
_____
_____
_____
_____
_____
_____
_____
_____
_____
_____
_____

DAY 10

⟁	**PURPLE**	Is used when God is speaking directly in the first person.
⟁	**GREEN**	Is used when a passage is talking about God speaking.
⟁	**GOLD**	Is used when God is speaking through non-verbal communication.
⟁	**BROWN**	Is used when Man is speaking on God's behalf in the Third Person.
⟁	**BLUE**	Is used for Angels speaking on God's behalf or a vision or a dream.
✳	**RED**	These are the Words of Jesus.

ACTS CHAPTER 10

1 There was a certain man in Caesarea called Cornelius, a centurion of the band called the Italian band,

2 A devout man, and one that feared God with all his house, which gave much alms to the people, and prayed to God always.

3 He saw in a vision evidently about the ninth hour of the day an angel of God coming in to him, and saying to him, Cornelius.

4 And when he looked on him, he was afraid, and said, What is it, Lord? And he said to him, Your prayers and your alms are come up for a memorial before God.

5 And now send men to Joppa, and call for one Simon, whose surname is Peter:

6 He lodges with one Simon a tanner, whose house is by the sea side: he shall tell you what you ought to do.

7 And when the angel which spoke to Cornelius was departed, he called two of his household servants, and a devout soldier of them that waited on him continually;

8 And when he had declared all these things to them, he sent them to Joppa.

9 On the morrow, as they went on their journey, and drew near to the city, Peter went up on the housetop to pray about the sixth hour:

10 And he became very hungry, and would have eaten: but while they made ready, he fell into a trance,

11 And saw heaven opened, and a certain vessel descending on him, as it had been a great sheet knit at the four corners, and let down to the earth:

12 Wherein were all manner of four footed beasts of the earth, and wild beasts, and creeping things, and fowls of the air.

13 And there came a voice to him, Rise, Peter; kill, and eat.

14 But Peter said, Not so, Lord; for I have never eaten anything that is common or unclean.

15 And the voice spoke to him again the second time, What God has cleansed, that call not you common.

VISIONS EVEN COME TO GENTILE.

God came to Cornelius in a vision. This vision includes an angel speaking to Cornelius. God is not a respecter of persons.

16 This was done thrice: and the vessel was received up again into heaven.

17 Now while Peter doubted in himself what this vision which he had seen should mean, behold, the men which were sent from Cornelius had made enquiry for Simon's house, and stood before the gate,

18 And called, and asked whether Simon, which was surnamed Peter, were lodged there.

19 While Peter thought on the vision, the Spirit said to him, Behold, three men seek you.

20 Arise therefore, and get you down, and go with them, doubting nothing: for I have sent them.

21 Then Peter went down to the men which were sent to him from Cornelius; and said, Behold, I am he whom you seek: what is the cause why you are come?

22 And they said, Cornelius the centurion, a just man, and one that fears God, and of good report among all the nation of the Jews, was warned from God by an holy angel to send for you into his house, and to hear words of you.

23 Then called he them in, and lodged them. And on the morrow Peter went away with them, and certain brothers from Joppa accompanied him.

24 And the morrow after they entered into Caesarea. And Cornelius waited for them, and he had called together his kinsmen and near friends.

25 And as Peter was coming in, Cornelius met him, and fell down at his feet, and worshipped him.

26 But Peter took him up, saying, Stand up; I myself also am a man.

27 And as he talked with him, he went in, and found many that were come together.

DAY 10

PURPLE	Is used when God is speaking directly in the first person.	
GREEN	Is used when a passage is talking about God speaking.	
GOLD	Is used when God is speaking through non-verbal communication.	
BROWN	Is used when Man is speaking on God's behalf in the Third Person.	
BLUE	Is used for Angels speaking on God's behalf or a vision or a dream.	
RED	These are the Words of Jesus.	

28 And he said to them, You know how that it is an unlawful thing for a man that is a Jew to keep company, or come to one of another nation; but God has showed me that I should not call any man common or unclean.

29 Therefore came I to you without gainsaying, as soon as I was sent for: I ask therefore for what intent you have sent for me?

30 And Cornelius said, Four days ago I was fasting until this hour; and at the ninth hour I prayed in my house, and, behold, a man stood before me in bright clothing,

31 And said, Cornelius, your prayer is heard, and your alms are had in remembrance in the sight of God.

32 Send therefore to Joppa, and call here Simon, whose surname is Peter; he is lodged in the house of one Simon a tanner by the sea side: who, when he comes, shall speak to you.

33 Immediately therefore I sent to you; and you have well done that you are come. Now therefore are we all here present before God, to hear all things that are commanded you of God.

34 Then Peter opened his mouth, and said, Of a truth I perceive that God is no respecter of persons:

35 But in every nation he that fears him, and works righteousness, is accepted with him.

36 The word which God sent to the children of Israel, preaching peace by Jesus Christ: (he is Lord of all:)

37 That word, I say, you know, which was published throughout all Judaea, and began from Galilee, after the baptism which John preached;

38 How God anointed Jesus of Nazareth with the Holy Ghost and with power: who went about doing good, and healing all that were oppressed of the devil; for God was with him.

39 And we are witnesses of all things which he did both in the land of the Jews, and in Jerusalem; whom they slew and hanged on a tree:

40 Him God raised up the third day, and showed him openly;

PETER'S VISION

Peter had been one of Jesus' apostles, and this vision shook Peter. God was telling Peter to accept the Gentiles into the faith, but the voice of God in this passage seemed to contradict scripture. God told Peter to eat things that the Old Testament forbids the people of God to eat. (Acts 10:10-18)

41 Not to all the people, but to witnesses chosen before God, even to us, who did eat and drink with him after he rose from the dead.

42 And he commanded us to preach to the people, and to testify that it is he which was ordained of God to be the Judge of quick and dead.

43 To him give all the prophets witness, that through his name whoever believes in him shall receive remission of sins.

44 While Peter yet spoke these words, the Holy Ghost fell on all them which heard the word.

45 And they of the circumcision which believed were astonished, as many as came with Peter, because that on the Gentiles also was poured out the gift of the Holy Ghost.

46 For they heard them speak with tongues, and magnify God. Then answered Peter,

47 Can any man forbid water, that these should not be baptized, which have received the Holy Ghost as well as we?

48 And he commanded them to be baptized in the name of the Lord. Then prayed they him to tarry certain days.

SOME THINGS TO PONDER

1. What was Peter's hangup that would have kept him from being open to sharing the gospel with Cornelius?
   _____
   _____
   _____

2. We again have two visions in chapter 10. What are the similarities? Differences? _____
   _____
   _____

3. What was the purpose behind these visions? _____
   _____

4. In what way(s) would you like to have Jesus or an angel come and visit you in a vision? _____
   _____
   _____

LEARNING TO HEAR GOD - DAY 10 – WHAT IF I GET IT WRONG?

Is it possible to spend time listening to God and get it wrong? Absolutely, YES! Some will say, "OK, then I'm done with this." Doesn't that seem like an overreaction? That's like throwing the baby out with the bath water. Keep the baby, get rid of the dirty water. Anyone can figure out that logic. There are many factors that can play a part in us getting something wrong when we are listening. Here are just a few:

FAULTY THINKING:

1. We can listen more to and trust more in our fears than in God.

2. Sometimes our own will gets in the way. For example, we are in love with that thing and want it more than anything and it is all we think about, so we go to listen to God and our idol is all we see, so we assume God is telling us to get it.

3. Some are more directed by their soul and operate more out of their intellect, their emotions or their own stubborn will and are not in touch with the will of God, so they will block God's voice if it contradicts what is going on in their soul.

4. If we are holding onto sin in our lives, it can hinder our relationship with God and He will be silent until we repent.

5. If we are not obeying what He is telling us to do, sometimes God will not give us another instruction until we obey what He said to us before.

6. Sometimes we have allowed demonic voices into our lives and listen to them rather than God.

DAY 10   DAILY LESSON

WEEK 2 | LESSON 10

It is vitally important to make sure we are in a place with God where we are surrendered to His will and committed to obeying Him. We must repent of any sin we have been holding onto. We must lay down any idols that have become more important in our lives than God, and then we must listen.

Don't be afraid of getting it wrong. If you operate from fear of getting it wrong, you will struggle to become confident in hearing God. Test what you hear by looking at God's Word and seeing if what you heard lines up with scripture. Test what you hear by sharing it with friends, family or a spiritual leader whom you trust.

Ask God to confirm what He speaks to you if it is directional in any way. If God says, "I love you" or "witness to that person," you know that lines up with scripture. On the other hand, as you are learning to hear God, if you believe God is leading you to marry someone, then ask God to confirm it. If your friends and family say you are crazy for wanting to marry Catherine Zeta Jones, and if she is already married, then you probably let your own desires overpower God's voice. If you believe God is leading you to quit your job, again, ask for confirmation. We will deal with this more in the next session.

MAKING IT PERSONAL

1. Have you ever let your own desires get in the way of God's will to the point that you lost perspective? Explain.

_____

_____

2. Are you afraid of making a mistake? Has it kept you from writing something down as you were listening because you were afraid it wasn't God? _____

_____

3. Is there anything in your life that you did perfect the first time that you tried? What is your normal experience with new things? _____

_____

_____

_____

GOD SPEAKS   **56**   SECTION 2: WEEK 2 | LESSONS 8-14

DAY 10   DAILY LESSON

WEEK 2 | LESSON 10

TIME TO LISTEN

Write in the space below whatever God may be speaking to you. Don't censor it as you write. If a song comes to mind pay attention to the words and write them. If scripture, write down the reference or the verse, if random thoughts write them. If you see images in your mind write them. Afterward ask God for discernment as to what each thing means.

_____

_____

_____

_____

_____

_____

_____

_____

_____

_____

_____

_____

_____

_____

_____

_____

_____

_____

_____

_____

_____

_____

DAY 11

	PURPLE	Is used when God is speaking directly in the first person.
	GREEN	Is used when a passage is talking about God speaking.
	GOLD	Is used when God is speaking through non-verbal communication.
	BROWN	Is used when Man is speaking on God's behalf in the Third Person.
	BLUE	Is used for Angels speaking on God's behalf or a vision or a dream.
	RED	These are the Words of Jesus.

ACTS CHAPTER 11

1 And the apostles and brothers that were in Judaea heard that the Gentiles had also received the word of God.

2 And when Peter was come up to Jerusalem, they that were of the circumcision contended with him,

3 Saying, You went in to men uncircumcised, and did eat with them.

4 But Peter rehearsed the matter from the beginning, and expounded it by order to them, saying,

5 I was in the city of Joppa praying: and in a trance I saw a vision, A certain vessel descend, as it had been a great sheet, let down from heaven by four corners; and it came even to me:

6 On the which when I had fastened my eyes, I considered, and saw four footed beasts of the earth, and wild beasts, and creeping things, and fowls of the air.

7 And I heard a voice saying to me, Arise, Peter; slay and eat.

8 But I said, Not so, Lord: for nothing common or unclean has at any time entered into my mouth.

9 But the voice answered me again from heaven, What God has cleansed, that call not you common.

10 And this was done three times: and all were drawn up again into heaven.

11 And, behold, immediately there were three men already come to the house where I was, sent from Caesarea to me.

12 And the Spirit bade me go with them, nothing doubting. Moreover these six brothers accompanied me, and we entered into the man's house:

13 And he showed us how he had seen an angel in his house, which stood and said to him, Send men to Joppa, and call for Simon, whose surname is Peter;

14 Who shall tell you words, whereby you and all your house shall be saved.

15 And as I began to speak, the Holy Ghost fell on them, as on us at the beginning.

POST RESURRECTION NEW TESTAMENT PROPHETS

Agabus was at the church in Antioch. God revealed to him that a famine was coming, and it did. God often reveals things that will come to His prophets.

16 Then remembered I the word of the Lord, how that he said, John indeed baptized with water; but you shall be baptized with the Holy Ghost.

17 For as much then as God gave them the like gift as he did to us, who believed on the Lord Jesus Christ; what was I, that I could withstand God?

18 When they heard these things, they held their peace, and glorified God, saying, Then has God also to the Gentiles granted repentance to life.

19 Now they which were scattered abroad on the persecution that arose about Stephen traveled as far as Phenice, and Cyprus, and Antioch, preaching the word to none but to the Jews only.

20 And some of them were men of Cyprus and Cyrene, which, when they were come to Antioch, spoke to the Grecians, preaching the LORD Jesus.

21 And the hand of the Lord was with them: and a great number believed, and turned to the Lord.

22 Then tidings of these things came to the ears of the church which was in Jerusalem: and they sent forth Barnabas, that he should go as far as Antioch.

23 Who, when he came, and had seen the grace of God, was glad, and exhorted them all, that with purpose of heart they would hold to the Lord.

24 For he was a good man, and full of the Holy Ghost and of faith: and much people was added to the Lord.

25 Then departed Barnabas to Tarsus, for to seek Saul:

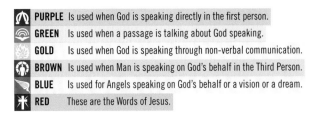

PURPLE Is used when God is speaking directly in the first person.
GREEN   Is used when a passage is talking about God speaking.
GOLD   Is used when God is speaking through non-verbal communication.
BROWN   Is used when Man is speaking on God's behalf in the Third Person.
BLUE   Is used for Angels speaking on God's behalf or a vision or a dream.
RED   These are the Words of Jesus.

26 And when he had found him, he brought him to Antioch. And it came to pass, that a whole year they assembled themselves with the church, and taught much people. And the disciples were called Christians first in Antioch.

27 And in these days came prophets from Jerusalem to Antioch.

28 And there stood up one of them named Agabus, and signified by the Spirit that there should be great dearth throughout all the world: which came to pass in the days of Claudius Caesar.

29 Then the disciples, every man according to his ability, determined to send relief to the brothers which dwelled in Judaea:

30 Which also they did, and sent it to the elders by the hands of Barnabas and Saul.

PERSONAL NOTES

DAY 11

DAILY LESSON

SOME THINGS TO PONDER

1. What was the people's response when Peter was telling his story of visions, angels and witnessing to the Gentiles?

_____

_____

2. How would you or your church respond to someone telling a similar experience? Why? _____

_____

_____

3. What was the evidence that God had accepted the Gentiles? _____

_____

_____

4. How did the church respond to the words of a prophet at the end of the chapter? _____

_____

_____

LEARNING TO HEAR GOD - DAY 11 – DIRECTIONAL GUIDANCE

God sometimes gives specific direction about where He wants us to go and what He wants us to do. Even the apostles wrestled with the things God told them. Peter had a vision where he ate all kinds of food forbidden in God's Word. As he waited on the Lord, the understanding became clearer. The vision was more about God accepting the Gentiles.

As long as I have been practicing hearing God's voice there are many times that I ask for confirmation. One night I had a dream where I was firing someone who worked for me. As I was finishing my morning bathroom routine I had a watch that the person had given me that was unbreakable shatter into many pieces. The Lord spoke clearly to my spirit that this relationship was being severed. I could not believe it. This was the furthest thing from my mind.

I began a fast for confirmation before I let him go. In my mind I had no reason. That same day that I began the fast he resigned. He was still telling me that he had my back, that this was an awesome ministry, and that I was a man of God, but he was saying something else to others. I didn't learn all that happened until his plan came crashing down on him and God showed me that what he meant for evil, God had worked out for my good.

DAY 11

DAILY LESSON

WEEK 2 | LESSON 11

Another time, God was speaking to me in every way possible that I was to go to Africa. I didn't want to and chalked everything up to coincidence. I had invitations from Africa, the people there wouldn't take no for an answer, God had told them I was coming. It didn't faze me. I had a prophet come tell me that I was going after a morning prayer for God to confirm if I was supposed to go. I still wasn't fazed. As I was spending time with the Lord, I knew he was speaking it to me, but I still asked for more confirmation.

I knew I would be gone from my family for weeks. I knew that we didn't have enough money in the ministry for me to go. I knew that my board of directors would oppose it for that reason. And quite frankly, that was not on my top 1000 things to do. However, I have now been many times and love Africa.

If we are willing to do whatever we hear when we listen to God, He will inevitably give us direction. If we ignore the direction, He may not speak to us much till we obey Him. Here are some valuable steps to remember:

1. Ask for confirmation.

2. Wait on Him for clarity and timing—remember Abraham.

3. Make sure it lines up with scripture.

4. Make sure your own desires don't get in the way of God's voice.

5. Obey when you know it is God and trust Him for the results.

6. Don't just run ahead with doing something that someone says God told them to tell you to do. Ask God if it is Him speaking through that person.

DAY 11

DAILY LESSON

WEEK 2 | LESSON 11

MAKING IT PERSONAL

1. Have you had someone tell you God told them to tell you something that was directional in nature? How did you respond? _____
_____
_____

2. Has God ever used you to tell someone something that they were to do? Describe an experience: _____
_____
_____

3. Have you ever had a dream where you were doing something that you wondered whether you were supposed to do it in real life? Explain: _____
_____
_____

4. Do you ever need specific direction from God that scripture is not specific about (like who to marry or where to go)? Do you believe He can give it? Why or why not? _____
_____
_____

TIME TO LISTEN

Write in the space below whatever God may be speaking to you. Don't censor it as you write. If a song comes to mind pay attention to the words and write them. If scripture, write down the reference or the verse, if random thoughts write them. If you see images in your mind write them. Afterward ask God for discernment as to what each thing means.

_____
_____
_____
_____
_____
_____
_____
_____
_____
_____
_____

TIME IN THE WORD

DAY 12

WEEK 2 | LESSON 12

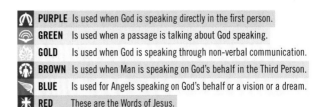

	PURPLE	Is used when God is speaking directly in the first person.
	GREEN	Is used when a passage is talking about God speaking.
	GOLD	Is used when God is speaking through non-verbal communication.
	BROWN	Is used when Man is speaking on God's behalf in the Third Person.
	BLUE	Is used for Angels speaking on God's behalf or a vision or a dream.
	RED	These are the Words of Jesus.

ACTS CHAPTER 12

1 Now about that time Herod the king stretched forth his hands to vex certain of the church.

2 And he killed James the brother of John with the sword.

3 And because he saw it pleased the Jews, he proceeded further to take Peter also. (Then were the days of unleavened bread.)

4 And when he had apprehended him, he put him in prison, and delivered him to four squads of soldiers to keep him; intending after Easter to bring him forth to the people.

5 Peter therefore was kept in prison: but prayer was made without ceasing of the church to God for him.

6 And when Herod would have brought him forth, the same night Peter was sleeping between two soldiers, bound with two chains: and the keepers before the door kept the prison.

7 And, behold, the angel of the Lord came on him, and a light shined in the prison: and he smote Peter on the side, and raised him up, saying, Arise up quickly. And his chains fell off from his hands.

8 And the angel said to him, Gird yourself, and bind on your sandals. And so he did. And he said to him, Cast your garment about you, and follow me.

9 And he went out, and followed him; and knew not that it was true which was done by the angel; but thought he saw a vision.

10 When they were past the first and the second ward, they came to the iron gate that leads to the city; which opened to them of his own accord: and they went out, and passed on through one street; and immediately the angel departed from him.

11 And when Peter was come to himself, he said, Now I know of a surety, that the LORD has sent his angel, and has delivered me out of the hand of Herod, and from all the expectation of the people of the Jews.

HOLY SPIRIT SPEAKS TO THE CHURCH

This passage tells us that The Holy Spirit spoke to the church. Now it is important to understand that "the church" refers to the people. The experience is not fully described. Did the Holy Spirit appear? Did one person hear the Holy Spirit and the others agree? Did everyone get the same or complimentary words as they listened to the Holy Spirit. (Acts 13:2)

12 And when he had considered the thing, he came to the house of Mary the mother of John, whose surname was Mark; where many were gathered together praying.

13 And as Peter knocked at the door of the gate, a damsel came to listen, named Rhoda.

14 And when she knew Peter's voice, she opened not the gate for gladness, but ran in, and told how Peter stood before the gate.

15 And they said to her, You are mad. But she constantly affirmed that it was even so. Then said they, It is his angel.

16 But Peter continued knocking: and when they had opened the door, and saw him, they were astonished.

17 But he, beckoning to them with the hand to hold their peace, declared to them how the Lord had brought him out of the prison. And he said, Go show these things to James, and to the brothers. And he departed, and went into another place.

18 Now as soon as it was day, there was no small stir among the soldiers, what was become of Peter.

19 And when Herod had sought for him, and found him not, he examined the keepers, and commanded that they should be put to death. And he went down from Judaea to Caesarea, and there stayed.

20 And Herod was highly displeased with them of

TIME IN THE WORD

DAY 12

WEEK 2 | LESSON 12

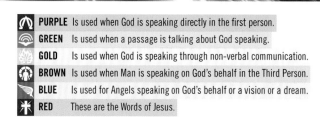

	PURPLE	Is used when God is speaking directly in the first person.
	GREEN	Is used when a passage is talking about God speaking.
	GOLD	Is used when God is speaking through non-verbal communication.
	BROWN	Is used when Man is speaking on God's behalf in the Third Person.
	BLUE	Is used for Angels speaking on God's behalf or a vision or a dream.
	RED	These are the Words of Jesus.

PAUL CURSES A SORCERER WITH BLINDNESS

The Holy Spirit led Paul to curse Elymas with blindness because he was blocking others from hearing God's Word. (Acts 13:9-11)

Tyre and Sidon: but they came with one accord to him, and, having made Blastus the king's chamberlain their friend, desired peace; because their country was nourished by the king's country.

21 And on a set day Herod, arrayed in royal apparel, sat on his throne, and made an oration to them.

22 And the people gave a shout, saying, It is the voice of a god, and not of a man.

23 And immediately the angel of the Lord smote him, because he gave not God the glory: and he was eaten of worms, and gave up the ghost.

24 But the word of God grew and multiplied.

25 And Barnabas and Saul returned from Jerusalem, when they had fulfilled their ministry, and took with them John, whose surname was Mark.

PERSONAL NOTES

_____
_____
_____
_____
_____
_____
_____
_____
_____
_____
_____
_____
_____
_____
_____
_____
_____
_____
_____
_____
_____
_____
_____
_____
_____
_____
_____
_____
_____
_____
_____
_____
_____
_____
_____

DAY 12

WEEK 2 | LESSON 12

DAILY LESSON

SOME THINGS TO PONDER

1. Are you surprised as you read Acts how many encounters there are with angels? Explain: _____
   _____
   _____

2. Why do you think Peter could have a literal encounter with an angel and yet think he was having a vision?
   _____
   _____

3. What roles did the angel play in this scenario? What did he communicate?
   _____
   _____

4. In the second encounter with an angel in verse 23, the angel doesn't say a word, but what do his actions
   communicate? What is the result? _____
   _____
   _____

LEARNING TO HEAR GOD - DAY 12 – HEARING GOD CORPORATELY

What if we hear God and someone else who hears God hears something that seems to contradict what we heard? When we live in the body of Christ and in a community of believers, this will inevitably happen. Several different things can be happening here. First, both people may have heard God and what seems to contradict actually makes sense to God; He will make that clear in time.

This happened with Paul and Agabus the prophet in Acts as well as people everywhere Paul went. Paul was compelled by God to go to Jerusalem. Agabus took Paul's belt and put it around his own waist and prophesied that prison chains awaited the person who wore that belt. The truth was that Paul already knew that but he knew he had to go. Many people tried to dissuade Paul because they knew he would be in prison. God had spoken to both Paul and Agabus, as well as other believers. Love constrained them to ask Paul not to go. Some may have even thought that Paul was ignoring the revelation God had given them.

Another possibility is that either Paul, Agabus or both of them have let something other than God's voice influence them. There were prophets in the Bible who got it wrong because a lying spirit had entered them. Sometimes our own intellect, training, or beliefs can keep us from hearing God more clearly.

I'm battling with this right now. A dear friend wants to move near us from another country. I know what I want and I also believe that I am hearing God say that this will happen. Because it is so personal and such a strong desire, it is easy for that to get in the way of really hearing God. On another front, I am so excited about The God Speaks Bible that I have a hard time discerning what comes from my enthusiasm and what comes from God. For this reason I tend to run so many things by my wife, my board and other close friends.

To hear God we need other people. There are times when God speaks clearly to us and no one will stand with us or be in agreement. That should not be the norm. There are also things God asks us to do that are not meant to be shared. However, most of the time it is godly and wise to seek the counsel of others.

PETER CAN'T TELL A VISON FROM REALITY

Peter's visions must have been so real that when an angel came to him, he couldn't tell if it was real or a vision. He finally realized that the angel was for real. (Acts 12:9)

MAKING IT PERSONAL

1. Have you ever experienced hearing God in a way that contradicted others? What happened? _____
   _____
   _____

2. Have you ever let personal desires or fears interfere with your ability to follow God? _____
   _____
   _____

3. Do you tend to believe your perspective and that what you hear is always correct or the opposite? What problems can either perspective cause? _____
   _____
   _____

DAY 12

DAILY LESSON

TIME TO LISTEN

Write in the space below whatever God may be speaking to you. Don't censor it as you write. If a song comes to mind pay attention to the words and write them. If scripture, write down the reference or the verse, if random thoughts write them. If you see images in your mind write them. Afterward ask God for discernment as to what each thing means.

TIME IN THE WORD

DAY 13

WEEK 2 | LESSON 13

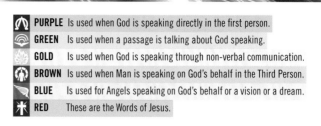

	PURPLE	Is used when God is speaking directly in the first person.
	GREEN	Is used when a passage is talking about God speaking.
	GOLD	Is used when God is speaking through non-verbal communication.
	BROWN	Is used when Man is speaking on God's behalf in the Third Person.
	BLUE	Is used for Angels speaking on God's behalf or a vision or a dream.
	RED	These are the Words of Jesus.

ACTS CHAPTER 13

1 Now there were in the church that was at Antioch certain prophets and teachers; as Barnabas, and Simeon that was called Niger, and Lucius of Cyrene, and Manaen, which had been brought up with Herod the tetrarch, and Saul.

2 As they ministered to the Lord, and fasted, the Holy Ghost said, Separate me Barnabas and Saul for the work whereunto I have called them.

3 And when they had fasted and prayed, and laid their hands on them, they sent them away.

4 So they, being sent forth by the Holy Ghost, departed to Seleucia; and from there they sailed to Cyprus.

5 And when they were at Salamis, they preached the word of God in the synagogues of the Jews: and they had also John to their minister.

6 And when they had gone through the isle to Paphos, they found a certain sorcerer, a false prophet, a Jew, whose name was Barjesus:

7 Which was with the deputy of the country, Sergius Paulus, a prudent man; who called for Barnabas and Saul, and desired to hear the word of God.

8 But Elymas the sorcerer (for so is his name by interpretation) withstood them, seeking to turn away the deputy from the faith.

9 Then Saul, (who also is called Paul,) filled with the Holy Ghost, set his eyes on him.

10 And said, O full of all subtlety and all mischief, you child of the devil, you enemy of all righteousness, will you not cease to pervert the right ways of the Lord?

11 And now, behold, the hand of the Lord is on you, and you shall be blind, not seeing the sun for a season. And immediately there fell on him a mist and a darkness; and he went about seeking some to lead him by the hand.

12 Then the deputy, when he saw what was done, believed, being astonished at the doctrine of the Lord.

13 Now when Paul and his company loosed from Paphos, they came to Perga in Pamphylia: and John departing from them returned to Jerusalem.

14 But when they departed from Perga, they came to

HOLDING ONTO PROMISES IN SCRIPTURE

Paul is declaring the promises of God that were fulfilled in Jesus. Jesus was the fulfillment of many promises. God is faithful to His promises. Find a promise of God today and hold onto it by trusting God to fulfill it. (Acts 13:32)

Antioch in Pisidia, and went into the synagogue on the sabbath day, and sat down.

15 And after the reading of the law and the prophets the rulers of the synagogue sent to them, saying, You men and brothers, if you have any word of exhortation for the people, say on.

16 Then Paul stood up, and beckoning with his hand said, Men of Israel, and you that fear God, give audience.

17 The God of this people of Israel chose our fathers, and exalted the people when they dwelled as stranger s in the land of Egypt, and with an high arm brought he them out of it.

18 And about the time of forty years suffered he their manners in the wilderness.

19 And when he had destroyed seven nations in the land of Chanaan, he divided their land to them by lot.

20 And after that he gave to them judges about the space of four hundred and fifty years, until Samuel the prophet.

21 And afterward they desired a king: and God gave to them Saul the son of Cis, a man of the tribe of Benjamin, by the space of forty years.

22 And when he had removed him, he raised up to them David to be their king; to whom also he gave their testimony, and said, I have found David the son of Jesse, a man after my own heart, which shall fulfill all my will.

23 Of this man's seed has God according to his promise raised to Israel a Savior, Jesus:

24 When John had first preached before his coming the baptism of repentance to all the people of Israel.

25 And as John fulfilled his course, he said, Whom

DAY 13

PURPLE	Is used when God is speaking directly in the first person.	
GREEN	Is used when a passage is talking about God speaking.	
GOLD	Is used when God is speaking through non-verbal communication.	
BROWN	Is used when Man is speaking on God's behalf in the Third Person.	
BLUE	Is used for Angels speaking on God's behalf or a vision or a dream.	
RED	These are the Words of Jesus.	

think you that I am? I am not he. But, behold, there comes one after me, whose shoes of his feet I am not worthy to loose.

26 Men and brothers, children of the stock of Abraham, and whoever among you fears God, to you is the word of this salvation sent.

27 For they that dwell at Jerusalem, and their rulers, because they knew him not, nor yet the voices of the prophets which are read every sabbath day, they have fulfilled them in condemning him.

28 And though they found no cause of death in him, yet desired they Pilate that he should be slain.

29 And when they had fulfilled all that was written of him, they took him down from the tree, and laid him in a sepulcher.

30 But God raised him from the dead:

31 And he was seen many days of them which came up with him from Galilee to Jerusalem, who are his witnesses to the people.

32 And we declare to you glad tidings, how that the promise which was made to the fathers,

33 God has fulfilled the same to us their children, in that he has raised up Jesus again; as it is also written in the second psalm, You are my Son, this day have I begotten you.

34 And as concerning that he raised him up from the dead, now no more to return to corruption, he said on this wise, I will give you the sure mercies of David.

35 Why he said also in another psalm, You shall not suffer your Holy One to see corruption.

36 For David, after he had served his own generation by the will of God, fell on sleep, and was laid to his fathers, and saw corruption:

37 But he, whom God raised again, saw no corruption.

38 Be it known to you therefore, men and brothers, that through this man is preached to you the forgiveness of sins:

39 And by him all that believe are justified from all things, from which you could not be justified by the law of Moses.

40 Beware therefore, lest that come on you, which is spoken of in the prophets;

41 Behold, you despisers, and wonder, and perish: for I work a work in your days, a work which you shall in no wise believe, though a man declare it to you.

42 And when the Jews were gone out of the synagogue, the Gentiles sought that these words might be preached to them the next sabbath.

43 Now when the congregation was broken up, many of the Jews and religious proselytes followed Paul and Barnabas: who, speaking to them, persuaded them to continue in the grace of God.

44 And the next sabbath day came almost the whole city together to hear the word of God.

45 But when the Jews saw the multitudes, they were filled with envy, and spoke against those things which were spoken by Paul, contradicting and blaspheming.

46 Then Paul and Barnabas waxed bold, and said, It was necessary that the word of God should first have been spoken to you: but seeing you put it from you, and judge yourselves unworthy of everlasting life, see, we turn to the Gentiles.

47 For so has the Lord commanded us, saying, I have set you to be a light of the Gentiles, that you should be for salvation to the ends of the earth.

48 And when the Gentiles heard this, they were glad, and glorified the word of the Lord: and as many as were ordained to eternal life believed.

49 And the word of the Lord was published throughout all the region.

50 But the Jews stirred up the devout and honorable women, and the chief men of the city, and raised persecution against Paul and Barnabas, and expelled them out of their coasts.

51 But they shook off the dust of their feet against them, and came to Iconium.

52 And the disciples were filled with joy, and with the Holy Ghost.

SOME THINGS TO PONDER

1. Who spoke in verse 2? What do you think it sounded like to the group of people who were fasting and praying in verse 2? _____
_____

2. Who was inspiring Paul's response to the sorcerer Elymas? What does Paul's response show us about the character of God? _____
_____
_____

3. What caused Sergius Paulus to believe the words that Paul was sharing? _____
_____
_____

4. What source did Paul use when he was preaching in the synagogues? _____
_____
_____

LEARNING TO HEAR GOD - DAY 13 – HEARING GOD TOGETHER IN MARRIAGE

Let's take things a step further in regards to hearing God in community, especially where it really can get sticky—in marriage. What if the wife hears something that the husband doesn't, or vice versa? I've heard many husbands say, "Tell her that she is supposed to submit to me." This reminds me of Balaam trying to get his donkey to move (see Numbers 22). The donkey could see the death angel about to take Balaam's life but Balaam (the prophet) was blind to the destruction awaiting him.

Can you see where I'm going with this illustration? In this story, even the donkey could see what the prophet didn't. I am not comparing our spouses to a donkey. Who was the bigger fool though in this story? I propose it was the quote "man of the house." Often when men want their wives to submit, the wife is actually seeing something that we are blind to. God is trying to use them to speak to us.

DAILY LESSON

When we get married, two become one, spiritually, before God. This may work well in heaven but here on earth it is often challenging. Marriage is the perfect place to refine hearing God in community. It takes great humility and it takes waiting. One person may be impulsive and wants to give a thousand dollars to a missionary, while the spouse is cautious, frugal, and knows their finances. Which one is hearing from God? Right now if there are 10 people in a room, half are agreeing with the giver and half with the thrifty spouse.

If God has brought us together and made the two one, could it be that God uses our spouse in our lives to balance us out? It is important to listen to, respect and honor our spouse as we learn to hear God's voice. If God tells you it is time to sell the house, move to Alaska and live in an igloo and your spouse doesn't agree, is it possible for God to also speak to your spouse?

Sometimes God gives us a vision but it isn't for now. We need to learn to wait upon the Lord and trust Him to speak to our spouses. I was recently ministering to a couple where the husband had spent years praying and listening to God. At first, his wife did not appear to be as "spiritual" as he was. It was incredible to watch the judgments of each other come down. They learned to hear God together and see how what God was speaking to the other could actually complement what they were hearing God say. This played no small part in the restoration of their marriage.

Hearing God together with our spouse takes humility, honor and respect. It is vital to listen to what our spouse is hearing. Don't rush ahead without praying together. If there are vast differences then wait upon the Lord. It may be that your spouse is being controlled by fear and you know it. Love your husband or wife, and really listen to them. Pray for any concerns and silently pray for God to set your spouse free from fear. It may be that God shows you that it is you who wasn't listening, or He may change your spouse's heart. Either way, the Lord is glorified through the character, love, unity and respect.

THINGS TO PONDER

If married, how often do you and your spouse hear slight variations on any given subject? _____
_____
_____

Have you judged your spouse or the opposite sex as less spiritually capable or more spiritually capable of hearing God? _____
_____
_____

DAY 13 LESSON REVIEW

WEEK 2 | LESSON 13

MAKING IT PERSONAL

1. What are some key principles in any relationship that are important if you are going to walk together and hear God in unity? _____
   _____
   _____

2. Have you judged the opposite sex in any way in regards to their spirituality? How could that affect your ability to listen and respect what they hear? _____
   _____
   _____

3. What was the spiritual environment like where you grew up? Who was the leader? How did your parents work through conflict and differences? _____
   _____
   _____

TIME TO LISTEN

Write in the space below whatever God may be speaking to you. Don't censor it as you write. If a song comes to mind pay attention to the words and write them. If scripture, write down the reference or the verse, if random thoughts write them. If you see images in your mind write them. Afterward ask God for discernment as to what each thing means.

_____
_____
_____
_____
_____
_____
_____
_____
_____
_____
_____
_____

	PURPLE	Is used when God is speaking directly in the first person.
	GREEN	Is used when a passage is talking about God speaking.
	GOLD	Is used when God is speaking through non-verbal communication.
	BROWN	Is used when Man is speaking on God's behalf in the Third Person.
	BLUE	Is used for Angels speaking on God's behalf or a vision or a dream.
	RED	These are the Words of Jesus.

ACTS CHAPTER 14

1 And it came to pass in Iconium, that they went both together into the synagogue of the Jews, and so spoke, that a great multitude both of the Jews and also of the Greeks believed.

2 But the unbelieving Jews stirred up the Gentiles, and made their minds evil affected against the brothers.

3 Long time therefore stayed they speaking boldly in the Lord, which gave testimony to the word of his grace, and granted signs and wonders to be done by their hands.

4 But the multitude of the city was divided: and part held with the Jews, and part with the apostles.

5 And when there was an assault made both of the Gentiles, and also of the Jews with their rulers, to use them spitefully, and to stone them,

6 They were aware of it, and fled to Lystra and Derbe, cities of Lycaonia, and to the region that lies round about:

7 And there they preached the gospel.

8 And there sat a certain man at Lystra, weak in his feet, being a cripple from his mother's womb, who never had walked:

9 The same heard Paul speak: who steadfastly beholding him, and perceiving that he had faith to be healed,

10 Said with a loud voice, Stand upright on your feet. And he leaped and walked.

11 And when the people saw what Paul had done, they lifted up their voices, saying in the speech of Lycaonia, The gods are come down to us in the likeness of men.

12 And they called Barnabas, Jupiter; and Paul, Mercurius, because he was the chief speaker.

13 Then the priest of Jupiter, which was before their city, brought oxen and garlands to the gates, and would have done sacrifice with the people.

14 Which when the apostles, Barnabas and Paul, heard of, they rent their clothes, and ran in among the people, crying out,

15 And saying, Sirs, why do you these things? We also are men of like passions with you, and preach to you that you should turn from these vanities to the living God, which made heaven, and earth, and the sea, and all things that are therein:

16 Who in times past suffered all nations to walk in their own ways.

17 Nevertheless he left not himself without witness, in that he did good, and gave us rain from heaven, and fruitful seasons, filling our hearts with food and gladness.

18 And with these sayings scarce restrained they the people, that they had not done sacrifice to them.

19 And there came thither certain Jews from Antioch and Iconium, who persuaded the people, and having stoned Paul, drew him out of the city, supposing he had been dead.

20 However,, as the disciples stood round about him, he rose up, and came into the city: and the next day he departed with Barnabas to Derbe.

21 And when they had preached the gospel to that city, and had taught many, they returned again to Lystra, and to Iconium, and Antioch,

22 Confirming the souls of the disciples, and exhorting them to continue in the faith, and that we must through much tribulation enter into the kingdom of God.

23 And when they had ordained them elders in every church, and had prayed with fasting, they commended them to the Lord, on whom they believed.

24 And after they had passed throughout Pisidia, they came to Pamphylia.

25 And when they had preached the word in Perga, they went down into Attalia:

26 And there sailed to Antioch, from where they had been recommended to the grace of God for the work which they fulfilled.

27 And when they were come, and had gathered the church together, they rehearsed all that God had done with them, and how he had opened the door of faith to the Gentiles.

28 And there they stayed long time with the disciples.

TIME IN THE WORD

DAY 14

WEEK 2 | LESSON 14

SOME THINGS TO PONDER

1. What happened as the apostles preached God's Word that hindered their fruitfulness? (vs. 1-2)

_____

_____

2. What did God do to confirm that the preaching was from God and not from man? _____

_____

_____

3. Did everyone accept the miracles? Why or why not?

_____

_____

4. How did the apostles minister to this crippled man? How do you normally pray for someone who is sick or in need of a miracle? How does your way differ? _____

_____

_____

DAY 14

WEEK 2 | LESSON 14

DAILY LESSON

LEARNING TO HEAR GOD - DAY 14 – HEARING GOD IN OUR SLEEP – HOW EFFICIENT?

Have you ever had God speak to you in your dreams? What if God has tried to speak to you in your dreams but you never paid attention? It wasn't until I started asking God to speak to me that I even paid attention to my dreams. God spoke to many people through dreams throughout the Bible. Over time the Lord has spoken some significant things to me through dreams. When my son, Andrew, was working with me on some of the God Speaks Bible, he noticed how much God spoke in and through dreams. Since he loved to sleep, he asked God to speak to him in dreams. Immediately he began to have vivid and specific dreams.

One night Andrew had a dream about something in a friend's life and called to tell him. The friend was shocked and convicted as God revealed what was going on in their life. It caused this person to get right with God. The reason that Andrew called this person was because he believed God might be speaking to the person for a purpose.

Sometimes we have so many distractions that the only time we are still and without stimulation is in our sleep. So is important to begin to pay attention to our dreams. If possible, write them down. When I know God is speaking to me, I will try to write down as much detail right when I wake up from the dream. If I wait the dream can be forgotten.

Pay attention to detail. If I sent two people now into another room and told them to look at a painting and come back and tell me about the painting, one might come back and say, "I saw a beach scene." Any details? "You know, some sand, water, stuff like that." Another person might come back and begin to describe the picture in vivid detail, from the colors, to the seagulls, to the hammock in the shade to the three people sitting together and another person off to the side snorkeling. They could describe the kind of boat that was in the water and how many people

were on the boat and maybe even the city where the beach was found because of either the scenery or the signs.

When you pay attention to the details you will find that there can be a lot of meaning in them. First, ask God if this dream is Him speaking to you. If you sense that it is from Him, write down what you first think that it means. Send a copy to someone you respect and ask them for their feedback and interpretation. I actually have a few friends who I respect and admire whom I send my dreams to. They always have incredible feedback. Just like, Daniel and Joseph, some people have a greater gift for dream interpretation than others. That is why we need each other.

I once had a dream where I was buying a home in another state and establishing a church in that home. The dream was vivid and I believed that it might actually happen someday. I have not seen that exact home as I have travelled in that state but I remember it, even though it was 10 years ago. I have ministered much there and know that His church has grown there. God may reveal something concrete that is really a symbol, or He may reveal something that will happen in the future.

Wait upon the Lord for His timing before waking up from a dream and putting your house up for sale. Pay attention, though. Sometimes God will speak to us and want action immediately. Let the Lord, make it clear to you. Feel free to ask for confirmation. The key is to be willing to do whatever the Lord asks and to obey.

DAY 14

DAILY LESSON

MAKING IT PERSONAL

1. Have you ever written out your dreams? How often? Why? _____
_____
_____

2. Do you remember a dream where you believe God spoke to you? Describe it. _____
_____
_____

3. Do you remember the interpretation of what God showed you in the dream? _____
_____
_____

TIME TO LISTEN

Write in the space below whatever God may be speaking to you. Don't censor it as you write. If a song comes to mind pay attention to the words and write them. If scripture, write down the reference or the verse, if random thoughts write them. If you see images in your mind write them. Afterward ask God for discernment as to what each thing means.

_____
_____
_____
_____
_____
_____
_____
_____
_____
_____
_____
_____
_____
_____
_____

GOD SPEAKS

LEARN HOW TO HEAR GOD

A JOURNEY THROUGH THE BOOK OF ACTS

SECTION
3

WEEK 3 | LESSONS 15-21
STUDY GUIDE

WEEK 3 | LESSONS 15-21

HINDRANCES TO HEARING – REMOVING THE ROADBLOCKS

Every Sunday in the fall the majority of wives know what it is like to have hindrances to hearing. It is a constant that many women face with the men in their lives, but it is particularly exacerbated on Sunday mornings by twenty-two men running around a field with lines all over it chasing whoever has a funny shaped brown orb. At least that is how many women see what is happening. We guys know the real value in this amazing sport called football. In front of a game is not typically the best place to engage in any meaningful conversation with a guy unless it has to do with play routes, drafts, fantasy brackets or if you can bring them some more food. Sorry, ladies. In the same way, when someone is sitting at a computer, or wearing headphones, or reading, watching their show, or talking on the phone, etc., etc., it is not a good time to engage them in conversation. When is the average American not doing one of the preceding things?

Can't you tell when the person on the other end of the line is doing something else and not hearing a word you are saying? How does that make you feel? Do you want to hang up the phone? The reason I'm asking is that I am terrible about that. I've worked on it a lot but my wife always nails me on it. She'll sweetly say, "Are you looking at your computer' or "what are you working on?" I know that it is frustrating but she handles it so well. There are so many distractions and hindrances in our lives today to hearing God's voice. My list will not be a complete list but I will seek to help you deal with as many of the main hindrances as possible. Ready?

UNBELIEF AND WRONG BELIEF

The first and greatest hurdle that many people face has to do with not believing that God is talking, can talk, or at least that He won't talk to "me." For many this belief is either taught to them at their church or it is built upon their experience of wanting to hear God, trying to hear God and getting only silence.

I'm sure you have felt it before. You pray and ask God for an answer and all you get is an empty room and silence. If that were your normal experience it would be impossible to keep trying. Normally this silence is based upon these hindrances, but God is passionately wanting to commune with you.

God speaks to unbelievers and the unsaved but God seldom answers anyone's challenge to prove Himself. God often requires faith first and then He moves, speaks and answers our prayers. I didn't begin to see God do miracles in my life and ministry when I wanted to. I began to see them when I began to believe that God would do those things and stepped out in faith.

For many people they don't have a hard time believing that God can speak or would speak. They struggle believing that He would ever have a reason to talk to them. For some it is shame and fear that they've sinned too much. Others think they are too insignificant for God to want to waste His valuable time talking to them. How sad. These are the lies that satan wants you to believe. I've so often seen God speak of His amazing love to these people and they can't believe it is God. They think it is something they have made up from what they want God to say to them. I know it is God because they would never come up with such loving expressions for themselves.

DISOBEDIENCE

God's patience and grace for us is so incredibly vast, we cannot fathom it. Yet, God can be angry; we can push His grace to the limit. I remember a time when I was willfully walking in disobedience to God. I avoided prayer because I knew what God wanted and I knew conviction would come. I was a teen and I avoided talking to my parents because I felt guilt. It was the break in those two relationships that meant a lot to me that motivated me to change something that I liked very much. Just a week or two of broken fellowship led me to break up with possibly the prettiest girl in the school, giving up what little chance I had of being in the "in crowd." That was a big choice as a 16-year-old, but I never looked back with regret. It was one of the best choices I ever made.

That is what sin does to us. It causes a rift in our walk with God that can eat away at our soul and keep us from even desiring fellowship. Besides outright sin, we can also neglect to obey God and do what He asks us to do. That will also affect our fellowship. If we know that God is calling us to do something but we refuse to, sometimes God will just wait until we are ready to listen and obey. Isaiah knew how to hear God and was not disobedient to speak what God told him to speak. That is what made him such an outstanding prophet.

Isaiah 50:4-5 "The Lord GOD has given me the tongue of the learned, that I should know how to speak a word in season to him that is weary: he wakens morning by morning, he wakens my ear to hear as the learned. The Lord GOD has opened my ear, and I was not rebellious, neither turned away back."

NOT LISTENING

With all the opening illustrations of men not listening to their wives, you would think I would have started there. Not listening is big a problem. We have a million excuses. Work was so demanding this week that I didn't have time. I have to chase that three-year-old around all day and I end the day collapsing into bed. I had to play four hours of my favorite game and listen to my new downloads from iTunes while watching my five favorite shows. When do you think I could find time to do nothing but listen – Hello!

Jeremiah 25:4 "And the LORD has sent to you all his servants the prophets, rising early and sending them; but you have not listened, nor inclined your ear to hear."

We can fail to listen because other things are priorities in our lives. But there is nothing more important than communing with God. It is amazing how upside down and backwards our priorities can be. That is not the only reason we fail to listen to God. Sometimes we don't listen because we are afraid of what He will tell us. Some fear that God will ask them to go to the garbage dumps in Manila or to Siberia. Some fear He will ask them to break up with that person they are dating, or stop that thing they are doing. Some believe God is just plain cruel and a killjoy.

God lets us rebel even if it hurts us because He is not controlling. When God says something to us it is because He loves us. I will never forget praying for a girl in New York. She was a cute young teenage girl. She had a necklace on and a ring on the necklace. I wouldn't have noticed it but the Lord told me that it belonged to a guy who was abusing her and that she was in bondage to this destructive relationship. I told her what God said to me and she began to cry. I told her that she didn't deserve to be treated that way and how much God loved her to tell her that. She pulled off the necklace and the ring, and for the rest of the night she was beaming with joy and freedom. It was listening and obeying that brought joy.

Sometimes it is not necessarily rebellion; we just don't make it a priority to take the time to listen to His voice. If we are truly honest, we would have to admit that other things are more important to us. We have to make it a priority and put everything below our communion with God. If it means using our lunch break, getting by with less sleep, turning off the TV, or dedicating another time, it is more important and more valuable to listen to God and read His Word than anything else we could do.

PRIDE

God is drawn toward the meek and will instruct them, but He resists the proud. (Psalm 25:9, James 4:6 and 1 Peter 5:5) Our pride will often fool us into thinking that we have heard God when in reality we are running ahead with our own plans and will. Our pride will also make it difficult for us to walk in fellowship with others. If we know that what we heard is God's will and anyone who doesn't see it the way we see it is not hearing God, we will be quick to judge. Agabus in Acts was a wonderful example of humility in hearing God. He is the most talked-about New Testament prophet. When He warned Paul about going to Jerusalem, there is no indication of him seeking to control Paul's action, no, "I told you so." He merely delivered the message and left the response up to God.

WEEK 3 | LESSONS 15-21
HINDRANCES TO HEARING – REMOVING THE ROADBLOCKS

When people believe that they alone have heard from God and everyone who doesn't agree with them is wrong, I call it the Elijah syndrome. At one point Elijah thought he was the only prophet of God left. God reminded him that He still had 4000 in Israel. That had to put Elijah back in his place. I think it would also be important to note that we don't have any prophesies recorded for most of those 4000 prophets, but they were prophets and they were prophesying. That illustrates that God was speaking all over the place, and of all the scripture related to God speaking, they make up only a small fraction of all the times and ways God speaks or has spoken.

Hearing God well, especially as it relates to what others are hearing, requires humility; our pride can have serious side effects when it comes to listening to God as well.

THE CURSES OF THIS WORLD

Worry can become all-consuming. It is the opposite of faith. Both faith and fear are projections into the future.

Neither one has to do with what we are experiencing in the moment. They are both based upon what we expect to experience and have a profound impact on what we are experiencing and will experience. If we spend our emotional energy expecting horrible things to happen and get caught up in the cares of this life, we will set our minds on what could go wrong.

Ever talk to people who are caught up in irrational fear? You can't get a word of sense into the mix without them shooting it down with their reason for fear. If we are so busy being caught up in our worry, we won't be listening to God. It can take on so many different forms. For some it is not the outright worry; it is more insidious than that. They work seventy hours a week because of secret fears that they will not have enough. Those fears don't feel like fear, they are called motivation and excellence. But beneath the surface is the true driving force—worry.

	PURPLE	Is used when God is speaking directly in the first person.
	GREEN	Is used when a passage is talking about God speaking.
	GOLD	Is used when God is speaking through non-verbal communication.
	BROWN	Is used when Man is speaking on God's behalf in the Third Person.
	BLUE	Is used for Angels speaking on God's behalf or a vision or a dream.
	RED	These are the Words of Jesus.

ACTS CHAPTER 15

1 And certain men which came down from Judaea taught the brothers, and said, Except you be circumcised after the manner of Moses, you cannot be saved.

2 When therefore Paul and Barnabas had no small dissension and disputation with them, they determined that Paul and Barnabas, and certain other of them, should go up to Jerusalem to the apostles and elders about this question.

3 And being brought on their way by the church, they passed through Phenice and Samaria, declaring the conversion of the Gentiles: and they caused great joy to all the brothers.

4 And when they were come to Jerusalem, they were received of the church, and of the apostles and elders, and they declared all things that God had done with them.

5 But there rose up certain of the sect of the Pharisees which believed, saying, That it was needful to circumcise them, and to command them to keep the law of Moses.

6 And the apostles and elders came together for to consider of this matter.

7 And when there had been much disputing, Peter rose up, and said to them, Men and brothers, you know how that a good while ago God made choice among us, that the Gentiles by my mouth should hear the word of the gospel, and believe.

8 And God, which knows the hearts, bore them witness, giving them the Holy Ghost, even as he did to us;

9 And put no difference between us and them, purifying their hearts by faith.

10 Now therefore why tempt you God, to put a yoke on the neck of the disciples, which neither our fathers nor we were able to bear?

11 But we believe that through the grace of the LORD Jesus Christ we shall be saved, even as they.

12 Then all the multitude kept silence, and gave audience to Barnabas and Paul, declaring what miracles

GIVING OF THE HOLY SPIRIT

a. The Holy Spirit was poured out on Cornelius and other gentiles (Acts 10:42-46)

b. Peter recounts the gentiles receiving the Holy Spirit as evidence that God accepts gentiles (Acts 11:15-16)

c. Jews testified that even gentiles received the Holy Spirit and this was the evidence they needed that God had accepted the gentiles (Acts 15:8)

d. In Ephesus, Paul laid hands on people to receive the Holy Spirit (Acts 19:6)

and wonders God had worked among the Gentiles by them.

13 And after they had held their peace, James answered, saying, Men and brothers, listen to me:

14 Simeon has declared how God at the first did visit the Gentiles, to take out of them a people for his name.

15 And to this agree the words of the prophets; as it is written,

16 After this I will return, and will build again the tabernacle of David, which is fallen down; and I will build again the ruins thereof, and I will set it up:

17 That the residue of men might seek after the Lord, and all the Gentiles, on whom my name is called, said the Lord, who does all these things.

18 Known to God are all his works from the beginning of the world.

19 Why my sentence is, that we trouble not them, which from among the Gentiles are turned to God:

20 But that we write to them, that they abstain from pollutions of idols, and from fornication, and from things strangled, and from blood.

21 For Moses of old time has in every city them that preach him, being read in the synagogues every sabbath day.

22 Then pleased it the apostles and elders with the whole church, to send chosen men of their own

PURPLE	Is used when God is speaking directly in the first person.
GREEN	Is used when a passage is talking about God speaking.
GOLD	Is used when God is speaking through non-verbal communication.
BROWN	Is used when Man is speaking on God's behalf in the Third Person.
BLUE	Is used for Angels speaking on God's behalf or a vision or a dream.
RED	These are the Words of Jesus.

company to Antioch with Paul and Barnabas; namely, Judas surnamed Barsabas and Silas, chief men among the brothers:

23 And they wrote letters by them after this manner; The apostles and elders and brothers send greeting to the brothers which are of the Gentiles in Antioch and Syria and Cilicia.

24 For as much as we have heard, that certain which went out from us have troubled you with words, subverting your souls, saying, You must be circumcised, and keep the law: to whom we gave no such commandment:

25 It seemed good to us, being assembled with one accord, to send chosen men to you with our beloved Barnabas and Paul,

26 Men that have hazarded their lives for the name of our Lord Jesus Christ.

27 We have sent therefore Judas and Silas, who shall also tell you the same things by mouth.

28 For it seemed good to the Holy Ghost, and to us, to lay on you no greater burden than these necessary things;

29 That you abstain from meats offered to idols, and from blood, and from things strangled, and from fornication: from which if you keep yourselves, you shall do well. Fare you well.

30 So when they were dismissed, they came to Antioch: and when they had gathered the multitude together, they delivered the letter:

31 Which when they had read, they rejoiced for the consolation.

32 And Judas and Silas, being prophets also themselves, exhorted the brothers with many words, and confirmed them.

33 And after they had tarried there a space, they were let go in peace from the brothers to the apostles.

34 Notwithstanding it pleased Silas to abide there still.

35 Paul also and Barnabas continued in Antioch, teaching and preaching the word of the Lord, with many others also.

36 And some days after Paul said to Barnabas, Let us go again and visit our brothers in every city where we have preached the word of the LORD, and see how they do.

37 And Barnabas determined to take with them John, whose surname was Mark.

38 But Paul thought not good to take him with them, who departed from them from Pamphylia, and went not with them to the work.

39 And the contention was so sharp between them, that they departed asunder one from the other: and so Barnabas took Mark, and sailed to Cyprus;

40 And Paul chose Silas, and departed, being recommended by the brothers to the grace of God.

41 And he went through Syria and Cilicia, confirming the churches.

PERSONAL NOTES

_____
_____
_____
_____
_____
_____
_____
_____
_____
_____
_____
_____
_____
_____
_____
_____
_____
_____
_____
_____

TIME IN THE WORD

DAY 15

WEEK 3 | LESSON 15

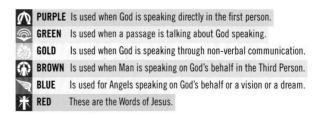

PURPLE Is used when God is speaking directly in the first person.
GREEN Is used when a passage is talking about God speaking.
GOLD Is used when God is speaking through non-verbal communication.
BROWN Is used when Man is speaking on God's behalf in the Third Person.
BLUE Is used for Angels speaking on God's behalf or a vision or a dream.
RED These are the Words of Jesus.

SOME THINGS TO PONDER

1. What did God do to bear witness to the Jewish believers that the conversion of the gentiles was real?

_____

_____

2. Who did God use to bring the message to the gentile converts of the decisions that the council had made regarding what gentiles were required to do? What was their gift and office in the church?

_____

_____

3. What caused a sharp dispute between Paul and Barnabas? What was the result? Why didn't they just listen to the Lord and do what God wanted? Or did they?

_____

_____

LEARNING TO HEAR GOD - DAY 15 – DIVINE VISITATIONS

Acts begins with the resurrected Jesus giving the apostles their final commission before ascending to heaven, and then there is an angel talking to them, asking why they are looking up into heaven when Jesus is coming back again one day. If you look at the divine encounters in the book of Acts you will find that they were fairly common.

The ways that angels appear vary greatly. Many times they actually appear in visions. I believe a vision is when God peels back the veil and allows us to see the spiritual realm around us. Sometimes God even peels back the veil of time and allows us to see what will be in the future. So when we see an angel in a vision it is not necessarily any less real than when they are seen in person.

Another way that angels appear is in actual human form. Again, it is God peeling back the veil. Only this time God allows that which exists in the heavenly things to appear in human- like form. The reason I say human- like is that angels often display qualities that we can only envy. They can appear and disappear, rise into the clouds, strike people with blindness, exert super-human strength and more.

There are other divine encounters besides angels. Some have encountered Jesus himself, including Paul and his companions and John on the Isle of Patmos. I once had a vision where I encountered Jesus and it was as real as anyone I have ever been with, though I knew it was a vision.

No matter what type of church I go to, if I ask if anyone has seen an angel there are a number of hands that go up. I was with an unsaved police officer one day who said, he knows he saw an angel and he doesn't even believe in God or the Bible. He was at an accident and someone came and told them about a woman who was trapped. She would have died without this person who then disappeared. Angels are God's messengers to man. That is what the word angel means in Greek.

There are also fallen angels and false angels of light that masquerade as angels of God. It is more than curious that all the biblical angels have masculine names but if you buy an angel in a store you find that most of the angels are dainty females. There are also many New Age websites that talk about angels and communicating with angels. Nowhere in the Bible are we encouraged to seek guidance from angels or does an angel hang out with a person all the time.

Be open to God's messengers but be wise and discerning at the same time. If Jesus appears to you, make sure it is the Jesus of scripture and that His message fits with what you know of the Bible.

DAY 15

DAILY LESSON

WEEK 2 | LESSON 15

MAKING IT PERSONAL

1. Have you ever seen an angel? Describe your experience. Was it in real life? In a dream or a vision? _____

_____

_____

2. Do you struggle to believe someone else when they tell you they have encountered an angel? If you do, why is that? _____

_____

3. In Daniel 9 and 10 Gabriel shows up when Daniel is praying and fasting and says to him, "Oh man of high esteem." Just for fun: How do you think an angel might address you? Why? How would you like to be addressed?

_____

_____

_____

TIME TO LISTEN

Write in the space below whatever God may be speaking to you. Don't censor it as you write. If a song comes to mind pay attention to the words and write them. If scripture, write down the reference or the verse, if random thoughts write them. If you see images in your mind write them. Afterward ask God for discernment as to what each thing means.

_____

_____

_____

_____

_____

_____

_____

_____

_____

_____

_____

_____

_____

_____

DAY 16

PURPLE	Is used when God is speaking directly in the first person.	

PURPLE Is used when God is speaking directly in the first person.
GREEN Is used when a passage is talking about God speaking.
GOLD Is used when God is speaking through non-verbal communication.
BROWN Is used when Man is speaking on God's behalf in the Third Person.
BLUE Is used for Angels speaking on God's behalf or a vision or a dream.
RED These are the Words of Jesus.

ACTS CHAPTER 16

1 Then came he to Derbe and Lystra: and, behold, a certain disciple was there, named Timotheus, the son of a certain woman, which was a Jewess, and believed; but his father was a Greek:

2 Which was well reported of by the brothers that were at Lystra and Iconium.

3 Him would Paul have to go forth with him; and took and circumcised him because of the Jews which were in those quarters: for they knew all that his father was a Greek.

4 And as they went through the cities, they delivered them the decrees for to keep, that were ordained of the apostles and elders which were at Jerusalem.

5 And so were the churches established in the faith, and increased in number daily.

6 Now when they had gone throughout Phrygia and the region of Galatia, and were forbidden of the Holy Ghost to preach the word in Asia,

7 After they were come to Mysia, they assayed to go into Bithynia: but the Spirit suffered them not.

8 And they passing by Mysia came down to Troas.

9 And a vision appeared to Paul in the night; There stood a man of Macedonia, and prayed him, saying, Come over into Macedonia, and help us.

10 And after he had seen the vision, immediately we endeavored to go into Macedonia, assuredly gathering that the Lord had called us for to preach the gospel to them.

11 Therefore loosing from Troas, we came with a straight course to Samothracia, and the next day to Neapolis;

12 And from there to Philippi, which is the chief city of that part of Macedonia, and a colony: and we were in that city abiding certain days.

13 And on the sabbath we went out of the city by a river side, where prayer was wont to be made; and we sat down, and spoke to the women which resorted thither.

14 And a certain woman named Lydia, a seller of purple,

GOD SPEAKS THROUGH AN EATHQUAKE
Paul and Silas were bound in prison. God used a different method this time to set them free. This time God sent an earthquake. (Acts 16:26)

HOLY SPIRIT FORBIDS PAUL TO PREACH IN ASIA
Paul was somehow told by the Holy Spirit not to go to Asia. God had other plans. (Acts 16:6)

of the city of Thyatira, which worshipped God, heard us: whose heart the Lord opened, that she attended to the things which were spoken of Paul.

15 And when she was baptized, and her household, she sought us, saying, If you have judged me to be faithful to the Lord, come into my house, and abide there. And she constrained us.

16 And it came to pass, as we went to prayer, a certain damsel possessed with a spirit of divination met us, which brought her masters much gain by soothsaying:

17 The same followed Paul and us, and cried, saying, These men are the servants of the most high God, which show to us the way of salvation.

18 And this did she many days. But Paul, being grieved, turned and said to the spirit, I command you in the name of Jesus Christ to come out of her. And he came out the same hour.

19 And when her masters saw that the hope of their gains was gone, they caught Paul and Silas, and drew them into the marketplace to the rulers,

20 And brought them to the magistrates, saying, These men, being Jews, do exceedingly trouble our city,

21 And teach customs, which are not lawful for us to receive, neither to observe, being Romans.

22 And the multitude rose up together against them: and

DAY 16

	PURPLE	Is used when God is speaking directly in the first person.
	GREEN	Is used when a passage is talking about God speaking.
	GOLD	Is used when God is speaking through non-verbal communication.
	BROWN	Is used when Man is speaking on God's behalf in the Third Person.
	BLUE	Is used for Angels speaking on God's behalf or a vision or a dream.
	RED	These are the Words of Jesus.

the magistrates rent off their clothes, and commanded to beat them.

23 And when they had laid many stripes on them, they cast them into prison, charging the jailor to keep them safely:

24 Who, having received such a charge, thrust them into the inner prison, and made their feet fast in the stocks.

25 And at midnight Paul and Silas prayed, and sang praises to God: and the prisoners heard them.

26 And suddenly there was a great earthquake, so that the foundations of the prison were shaken: and immediately all the doors were opened, and everyone's bands were loosed.

27 And the keeper of the prison awaking out of his sleep, and seeing the prison doors open, he drew out his sword, and would have killed himself, supposing that the prisoners had been fled.

28 But Paul cried with a loud voice, saying, Do yourself no harm: for we are all here.

29 Then he called for a light, and sprang in, and came trembling, and fell down before Paul and Silas,

30 And brought them out, and said, Sirs, what must I do to be saved?

31 And they said, Believe on the Lord Jesus Christ, and you shall be saved, and your house.

32 And they spoke to him the word of the Lord, and to all that were in his house.

33 And he took them the same hour of the night, and washed their stripes; and was baptized, he and all his, straightway.

34 And when he had brought them into his house, he set meat before them, and rejoiced, believing in God with all his house.

35 And when it was day, the magistrates sent the sergeants, saying, Let those men go.

36 And the keeper of the prison told this saying to Paul,

MACEDONEAN VISION

God spoke to Paul through a vision. In the vision a man was calling Paul to come to Macedonia. Sometimes God leads through a vision. (Acts 16:9-10)

The magistrates have sent to let you go: now therefore depart, and go in peace.

37 But Paul said to them, They have beaten us openly uncondemned, being Romans, and have cast us into prison; and now do they thrust us out privately? no truly; but let them come themselves and fetch us out.

38 And the sergeants told these words to the magistrates: and they feared, when they heard that they were Romans.

39 And they came and sought them, and brought them out, and desired them to depart out of the city.

40 And they went out of the prison, and entered into the house of Lydia: and when they had seen the brothers, they comforted them, and departed.

PERSONAL NOTES

_____

_____

_____

_____

_____

_____

_____

_____

_____

_____

_____

_____

_____

_____

_____

_____

TIME IN THE WORD

DAY 16

WEEK 3 | LESSON 16

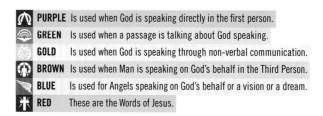

PURPLE	Is used when God is speaking directly in the first person.
GREEN	Is used when a passage is talking about God speaking.
GOLD	Is used when God is speaking through non-verbal communication.
BROWN	Is used when Man is speaking on God's behalf in the Third Person.
BLUE	Is used for Angels speaking on God's behalf or a vision or a dream.
RED	These are the Words of Jesus.

SOME THINGS TO PONDER

1. What/who hindered the apostles from going into Asia and Bythinia? What do you think that was like?

   _____

   _____

2. No one, that I recall, in the bible ever describes what it is like to be led by the Holy Spirit or directed by the Holy Spirit or hindered by the Holy Spirit. How does someone know if the Holy Spirit is speaking or not?

   _____

   _____

3. What does God use to lead the apostles to Macedonia? How serious did the apostles take this form of God speaking? _____

   _____

4. What did God say about the imprisonment of Paul and Silas? How did He speak? _____

   _____

   _____

LEARNING TO HEAR GOD - DAY 16 – OBEY TO HEAR

It is vital that we obey the direction that God gives us if we want to continuously hear His voice. At one time in my journey of listening to God's voice I would wake up every morning and spend hours listening, and I was getting direction and revelation from the Lord. I had spent several years learning how to listen. I had asked the Lord to disciple me. Every morning it was the same. Then one day I noticed something. It had been about a week and I wasn't hearing God speak at all for that week.

I had taken for granted that God would speak to me this way for the rest of my life. I asked the Lord what was happening and He told me that I was not obeying Him. For many months as the Lord spoke to me He would tell me to write what He was saying to me. "That was a great idea," I would respond with enthusiasm. I knew that what God was teaching me wasn't just for me. I was to write. But I was often too comfortable and didn't want a computer in front of me while I communed with the Lord. I also didn't believe I could write.

I took the Lord's command as a great idea, a worthwhile suggestion, but not seriously enough to put action to it.

As I got out my computer and began to journal what the Lord was speaking to me, the Lord continued to speak to me. From that time came a book called, "Lord, Disciple Me," which has since been revised and retitled, "The Jesus Training Manual". I have continued to write now for years as I sit in the Lord's presence. Writing for me was not a passion, or a desire, or something I ever thought that I would do. It was a mandate from God that I have grown to love.

The key is learning to obey God no matter what He asks. For some that is the greatest fear. Many believe if they give God a blank check for their lives that He will put them in the most miserable place on the planet. They don't trust His love and wisdom. Truth is, He might send you to the garbage dumps of Manila, but if He does, it will be the greatest place on earth for you. He probably won't, but you can trust Him. Maybe he wants you to write or sing for Him or teach a children's class at church. Just listen and obey. Sometimes He wants us to do nothing but be with Him.

Even now, I sit before the Lord and I ask Him, "What I should write today?"

I start most of my days at 5:00 a.m. with no distractions and no interruptions. I have about 2 hours of communion with the Lord daily. When there is more that the Lord wants to speak to me, He wakes me up at 4:00 or 3:00 and I am sustained during those days. I wouldn't trade this time with the Lord for anything, not even sleep. Sometimes, the Lord even says, "Sleep this morning. We will commune tomorrow." Even that sleep that He directs feels like time with Him.

King Saul at one point had disobeyed God and could no longer hear God's voice. He became foolish and went to a witch and paid for that mistake with his life and the life of his son. There are many things that can hinder us from hearing God and there can be serious consequences from not listening. We will take a look at some of those next.

DAY 16

DAILY LESSON

MAKING IT PERSONAL

1. Have you ever struggled to trust God and what He would ask of you? Explain: _____
   _____
   _____

2. Do you remember a time when the Lord called you to do something for Him? What was that like?
   _____
   _____
   _____

3. Is there something that God has spoken to you that you have not followed through on or obeyed Him regarding?
   _____
   _____

TIME TO LISTEN

Write in the space below whatever God may be speaking to you. Don't censor it as you write. If a song comes to mind pay attention to the words and write them. If scripture, write down the reference or the verse, if random thoughts write them. If you see images in your mind write them. Afterward ask God for discernment as to what each thing means.

_____
_____
_____
_____
_____
_____
_____
_____
_____
_____
_____
_____

DAY 17

	PURPLE	Is used when God is speaking directly in the first person.
	GREEN	Is used when a passage is talking about God speaking.
	GOLD	Is used when God is speaking through non-verbal communication.
	BROWN	Is used when Man is speaking on God's behalf in the Third Person.
	BLUE	Is used for Angels speaking on God's behalf or a vision or a dream.
	RED	These are the Words of Jesus.

ACTS: CHAPTER 17

1 Now when they had passed through Amphipolis and Apollonia, they came to Thessalonica, where was a synagogue of the Jews:

2 And Paul, as his manner was, went in to them, and three sabbath days reasoned with them out of the scriptures,

3 Opening and alleging, that Christ must needs have suffered, and risen again from the dead; and that this Jesus, whom I preach to you, is Christ.

4 And some of them believed, and consorted with Paul and Silas; and of the devout Greeks a great multitude, and of the chief women not a few.

5 But the Jews which believed not, moved with envy, took to them certain lewd fellows of the baser sort, and gathered a company, and set all the city on an uproar, and assaulted the house of Jason, and sought to bring them out to the people.

6 And when they found them not, they drew Jason and certain brothers to the rulers of the city, crying, These that have turned the world upside down are come here also;

7 Whom Jason has received: and these all do contrary to the decrees of Caesar, saying that there is another king, one Jesus.

8 And they troubled the people and the rulers of the city, when they heard these things.

9 And when they had taken security of Jason, and of the other, they let them go.

10 And the brothers immediately sent away Paul and Silas by night to Berea: who coming thither went into the synagogue of the Jews.

11 These were more noble than those in Thessalonica, in that they received the word with all readiness of mind, and searched the scriptures daily, whether those things were so.

12 Therefore many of them believed; also of honorable women which were Greeks, and of men, not a few.

BEREANS TEST PAUL'S MESSAGE

The Bereans were considered more noble because they received God's word readily and searched the scriptures for themselves. It is good to test everything by God's Word. (Acts 17:11)

13 But when the Jews of Thessalonica had knowledge that the word of God was preached of Paul at Berea, they came thither also, and stirred up the people.

14 And then immediately the brothers sent away Paul to go as it were to the sea: but Silas and Timotheus stayed there still.

15 And they that conducted Paul brought him to Athens: and receiving a commandment to Silas and Timotheus for to come to him with all speed, they departed.

16 Now while Paul waited for them at Athens, His Spirit was stirred in him, when he saw the city wholly given to idolatry.

17 Therefore disputed he in the synagogue with the Jews, and with the devout persons, and in the market daily with them that met with him.

18 Then certain philosophers of the Epicureans, and of the Stoicks, encountered him. And some said, What will this babbler say? other some, He seems to be a setter forth of strange gods: because he preached to them Jesus, and the resurrection.

19 And they took him, and brought him to Areopagus, saying, May we know what this new doctrine, whereof you speak, is?

20 For you bring certain strange things to our ears: we would know therefore what these things mean.

21 (For all the Athenians and strangers which were there spent their time in nothing else, but either to tell, or to hear some new thing.)

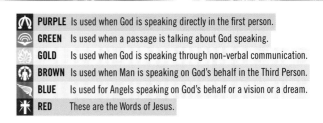

PURPLE	Is used when God is speaking directly in the first person.
GREEN	Is used when a passage is talking about God speaking.
GOLD	Is used when God is speaking through non-verbal communication.
BROWN	Is used when Man is speaking on God's behalf in the Third Person.
BLUE	Is used for Angels speaking on God's behalf or a vision or a dream.
RED	These are the Words of Jesus.

22 Then Paul stood in the middle of Mars' hill, and said, You men of Athens, I perceive that in all things you are too superstitious.

23 For as I passed by, and beheld your devotions, I found an altar with this inscription, TO THE UNKNOWN GOD. Whom therefore you ignorantly worship, him declare I to you.

24 God that made the world and all things therein, seeing that he is Lord of heaven and earth, dwells not in temples made with hands;

25 Neither is worshipped with men's hands, as though he needed anything, seeing he gives to all life, and breath, and all things;

26 And has made of one blood all nations of men for to dwell on all the face of the earth, and has determined the times before appointed, and the bounds of their habitation;

27 That they should seek the Lord, if haply they might feel after him, and find him, though he be not far from everyone of us:

28 For in him we live, and move, and have our being; as certain also of your own poets have said, For we are also his offspring.

29 For as much then as we are the offspring of God, we ought not to think that the Godhead is like to gold, or silver, or stone, graven by are and man's device.

30 And the times of this ignorance God winked at; but now commands all men everywhere to repent:

31 Because he has appointed a day, in the which he will judge the world in righteousness by that man whom he has ordained; whereof he has given assurance to all men, in that he has raised him from the dead.

32 And when they heard of the resurrection of the dead, some mocked: and others said, We will hear you again of this matter.

33 So Paul departed from among them.

34 However, certain men joined to him, and believed: among the which was Dionysius the Areopagite, and a woman named Damaris, and others with them.

GOD COMFRONTS PAUL BY SPEAKING IN A VISION

Paul often seemed to be running for his life. God told him that in Corinth he would be safe because God was with him and would not allow him to be hurt. (Acts 18:9-11)

PERSONAL NOTES

_____
_____
_____
_____
_____
_____
_____
_____
_____
_____
_____
_____
_____
_____
_____
_____
_____
_____
_____
_____
_____
_____
_____
_____
_____
_____

DAY 17

DAILY LESSON

SOME THINGS TO PONDER

1. How did the people of Thessalonica respond to Paul and Silas for preaching the Word of God and for doing what God told them to do? Is it possible for us to hear God and do what He tells us and experience the same?

   _____

   _____

   _____

2. What made the believers in Berea more noble than those in Thessalonica? Why? _____

   _____

   _____

   _____

3. What spirit is spoken of in verse 16? How did His Spirit impact Paul's direction? How is this different from the Holy Spirit or an evil spirit? _____

   _____

   _____

4. In Athens Paul used more logic and less scripture in his speaking. Even his speaking was not called preaching but disputing. Why do you think that is? Why not just do miracles here? _____

   _____

   _____

LEARNING TO HEAR HIM - DAY 17 – HINDRANCES TO HEARING GOD.

Many believers have heard God's voice but didn't know His voice, so they think they have never heard the Lord. Others have heard God before but are not able to hear the Lord now. There are many things that can keep us from hearing the Lord's voice. Today we will examine some of them and seek to remove any hindrances that stand in the way of us hearing God.

The first hindrance that many people deal with is faulty beliefs about hearing God. If you don't believe that God speaks today, then you probably won't hear Him. God has no need to prove himself. People often say things to God, like, "If you are there, show me a sign." God has already shown Himself.

Another hindrance is unconfessed sin in our lives. I remember once as a teen when God convicted me about something I was getting involved in. I couldn't talk about it with my parents and couldn't go to God. I knew what both would say. Stop it! I didn't want to hear that. The relationship with God and with my parents at that point stopped because I didn't want to hear them. I was missing the intimacy with God and the ability to talk to my parents. That is what led me to stop the sin and recommit to Christ being Lord.

DAY 17   DAILY LESSON

LEARNING TO HEAR HIM - DAY 17 – HINDRANCES TO HEARING GOD.

Sometimes, we have tuned God's voice out so long and so well and maintained our religious activity that we forget what it was like to hear God.

Not obeying the Lord will also hinder our ability to hear Him. You may ask, "How this is different from sin?" What I mean here is that sometimes God speaks to us, asks us to do something, or gives us direction and we ignore it. God may stop talking to us, not because we have done some evil thing but because we didn't do what He was asking us to do. Jonah stopped listening to the Lord and communing with God because He didn't want to go to Nineveh even though that is what the Lord kept asking him to do.

Husbands who don't treat their wives well can have their communion with God affected (1 Peter 3:7). When we are at odds with others, especially our spouse, it can hinder our prayers and our ability to listen to God. Bitterness can be all-consuming and totally distort our perspective on everything.

One of the greatest hindrances is not listening (Jeremiah 25:4). If we don't take time to listen then we won't hear. Many don't know that God is speaking to them, others are so distracted and busy that they don't have time for the most important relationship of all. Most don't know that they can or should be listening.

Pride can also keep us from hearing God (Psalm 25:9). Our pride can make us over-confident in ourselves and our own wisdom and decision making. David was one of the greatest warriors ever. There were almost no battles lost in all of his military career, but he would ask God for guidance daily. Saul, on the other hand, was impulsive and ran ahead without waiting on the Lord. That was his downfall.

Finally, the cares of this world can choke out our ability to hear God. If our minds are consumed with fears, worries or even good things like cars, houses and the things of this world, then we won't have time to listen. Jesus told us this would be the case in Luke 8 in the parable of the sower.

MAKING IT PERSONAL:

1. Which of these hindrances do you struggle with the most? Why? _____
   _____
   _____

2. Can you remember a time when you struggled with most of them at some time in your life? How did you overcome any of them? _____
   _____
   _____

3. Which hindrances do you see operating most often in those you are closest to? _____
   _____
   _____

DAY 17

DAILY LESSON

TIME TO LISTEN

Write in the space below whatever God may be speaking to you. Don't censor it as you write. If a song comes to mind pay attention to the words and write them. If scripture, write down the reference or the verse, if random thoughts write them. If you see images in your mind write them. Afterward ask God for discernment as to what each thing means.

_____

_____

_____

_____

_____

_____

_____

_____

_____

_____

_____

_____

_____

_____

_____

_____

_____

_____

_____

_____

_____

	PURPLE	Is used when God is speaking directly in the first person.
	GREEN	Is used when a passage is talking about God speaking.
	GOLD	Is used when God is speaking through non-verbal communication.
	BROWN	Is used when Man is speaking on God's behalf in the Third Person.
	BLUE	Is used for Angels speaking on God's behalf or a vision or a dream.
	RED	These are the Words of Jesus.

ACTS: CHAPTER 18

1 After these things Paul departed from Athens, and came to Corinth;

2 And found a certain Jew named Aquila, born in Pontus, lately come from Italy, with his wife Priscilla; (because that Claudius had commanded all Jews to depart from Rome:) and came to them.

3 And because he was of the same craft, he stayed with them, and worked: for by their occupation they were tentmakers.

4 And he reasoned in the synagogue every sabbath, and persuaded the Jews and the Greeks.

5 And when Silas and Timotheus were come from Macedonia, Paul was pressed in the spirit, and testified to the Jews that Jesus was Christ.

6 And when they opposed themselves, and blasphemed, he shook his raiment, and said to them, Your blood be on your own heads; I am clean; from now on I will go to the Gentiles.

7 And he departed there, and entered into a certain man's house, named Justus, one that worshipped God, whose house joined hard to the synagogue.

8 And Crispus, the chief ruler of the synagogue, believed on the Lord with all his house; and many of the Corinthians hearing believed, and were baptized.

9 Then spoke the Lord to Paul in the night by a vision, Be not afraid, but speak, and hold not your peace:

10 For I am with you, and no man shall set on you to hurt you: for I have much people in this city.

11 And he continued there a year and six months, teaching the word of God among them.

12 And when Gallio was the deputy of Achaia, the Jews made insurrection with one accord against Paul, and brought him to the judgment seat,

13 Saying, This fellow persuades men to worship God contrary to the law.

14 And when Paul was now about to open his mouth, Gallio said to the Jews, If it were a matter of wrong or wicked lewdness, O you Jews, reason would that I should bear with you:

15 But if it be a question of words and names, and of your law, look you to it; for I will be no judge of such matters.

16 And he drove them from the judgment seat.

17 Then all the Greeks took Sosthenes, the chief ruler of the synagogue, and beat him before the judgment seat. And Gallio cared for none of those things.

18 And Paul after this tarried there yet a good while, and then took his leave of the brothers, and sailed there into Syria, and with him Priscilla and Aquila; having shorn his head in Cenchrea: for he had a vow.

19 And he came to Ephesus, and left them there: but he himself entered into the synagogue, and reasoned with the Jews.

20 When they desired him to tarry longer time with them, he consented not;

21 But bade them farewell, saying, I must by all means keep this feast that comes in Jerusalem: but I will return again to you, if God will. And he sailed from Ephesus.

22 And when he had landed at Caesarea, and gone up, and saluted the church, he went down to Antioch.

23 And after he had spent some time there, he departed, and went over all the country of Galatia and Phrygia in order, strengthening all the disciples.

24 And a certain Jew named Apollos, born at Alexandria, an eloquent man, and mighty in the scriptures, came to Ephesus.

25 This man was instructed in the way of the Lord; and being fervent in the spirit, he spoke and taught diligently the things of the Lord, knowing only the baptism of John.

26 And he began to speak boldly in the synagogue: whom when Aquila and Priscilla had heard, they took him to them, and expounded to him the way of God more perfectly.

27 And when he was disposed to pass into Achaia, the brothers wrote, exhorting the disciples to receive him: who, when he was come, helped them much which had believed through grace:

28 For he mightily convinced the Jews, and that publicly, showing by the scriptures that Jesus was Christ.

	PURPLE	Is used when God is speaking directly in the first person.
	GREEN	Is used when a passage is talking about God speaking.
	GOLD	Is used when God is speaking through non-verbal communication.
	BROWN	Is used when Man is speaking on God's behalf in the Third Person.
	BLUE	Is used for Angels speaking on God's behalf or a vision or a dream.
	RED	These are the Words of Jesus.

SOME THINGS TO PONDER

1. Reread verses 4 and 5. What you will notice is that Paul went from reasoning every day in the synagogue to finally being compelled by His Spirit to testify that Jesus was the Christ. Why not start by preaching Jesus? _____

_____

_____

2. Why do you think God Himself spoke to Paul in a vision instead of through an angel, dream or prophet in verses 9-10? _____

_____

_____

3. Apollos was an eloquent man and mighty in the scriptures, but Aquila and Priscilla took him and taught him more. What does that tell us about the character of Apollos? Would you say that it is common for people who already know a lot and who are eloquent? How should we emulate that? _____

_____

_____

LEARNING TO HEAR HIM - DAY 18 – OUR GREAT HINDRANCE

One of the greatest hindrances to listening, hearing, and obeying God's voice is our own will. If God is going to communicate His will with us but we are not willing to listen, trust Him and obey, then we shut out the voice of God.

Many years ago, Scott Wesley Brown wrote a humorous song called, "Please don't send me to Africa." He put into words what many people fear. If I listen to God and surrender my life to Him, I know he will send me to Africa to be a missionary and I don't want to do that. Maybe your fear is not Africa, but many people fear God's will.

The thinking of some goes something like this, "God doesn't care about me or my happiness. All He cares about is those starving people and making me miserable." One person I have ministered to believed God was narcissistic and only cared about Himself, His glory, and making us miserable. This guy did more service in his church than almost anyone else and was miserable until God set him free.

Jeremiah 7:24 says, "But they did not listen or pay attention; instead, they followed the stubborn inclinations of their evil hearts." Many times we want to do our own thing, and God will let us. He doesn't make us do His will.

In order to hear God well and be in tune with His will and direction it is imperative that our hearts be in the right place of submission to God.

Our motives are essential as well. If we are out for self-glorification or fearful self-protection, either way, our self will get in the way of hearing God.

It is vital to get to the place of trusting God—that He cares about us—that He knows us and what is best for us. When God was leading me to go to Africa, I thought that there was no way. I didn't want to go. I wasn't listening. Thankfully, God knew that my heart was to do His will and He knew going to Africa would be a blessing to me. I didn't know that Africa would become one of my favorite places out of over 20 countries I've been to. I didn't foresee how incredible the people were and how exciting it would be to minister there. He did.

God isn't calling everyone to Africa. Where He is calling you is to Himself and to a life that is surrendered, in faith and trust, to Him and to His will. He wants to speak to you. He wants to lead you. He wants to give you the desires of your heart. Desires you don't even know you have right now. He loves you and has more for you than you could ever imagine.

Surrender your will to Him, listen to what He has to say, and obey.

John 10: 27 "My sheep hear My voice, and I know them and they follow Me."

DAY 18

DAILY LESSON

WEEK 3 | LESSON 18

MAKING IT PERSONAL:

1. What does this devotion suggest is the greatest hindrance to hearing God? Do you agree? Why or why not?

_____

_____

2. Can you remember a time when your desires or fears kept you from listening to or obeying God? Explain:

_____

_____

3. Are you at a place where you have come to trust God completely with your life and future? Explain:

_____

_____

TIME TO LISTEN

Write in the space below whatever God may be speaking to you. Don't censor it as you write. If a song comes to mind pay attention to the words and write them. If scripture, write down the reference or the verse, if random thoughts write them. If you see images in your mind write them. Afterward ask God for discernment as to what each thing means.

_____

_____

_____

_____

_____

_____

_____

_____

_____

_____

_____

_____

_____

PURPLE	Is used when God is speaking directly in the first person.
GREEN	Is used when a passage is talking about God speaking.
GOLD	Is used when God is speaking through non-verbal communication.
BROWN	Is used when Man is speaking on God's behalf in the Third Person.
BLUE	Is used for Angels speaking on God's behalf or a vision or a dream.
RED	These are the Words of Jesus.

ACTS: CHAPTER 19

1 And it came to pass, that, while Apollos was at Corinth, Paul having passed through the upper coasts came to Ephesus: and finding certain disciples,

2 He said to them, Have you received the Holy Ghost since you believed? And they said to him, We have not so much as heard whether there be any Holy Ghost.

3 And he said to them, To what then were you baptized? And they said, To John's baptism.

4 Then said Paul, John truly baptized with the baptism of repentance, saying to the people, that they should believe on him which should come after him, that is, on Christ Jesus.

5 When they heard this, they were baptized in the name of the Lord Jesus.

6 And when Paul had laid his hands on them, the Holy Ghost came on them; and they spoke with tongues, and prophesied.

7 And all the men were about twelve.

8 And he went into the synagogue, and spoke boldly for the space of three months, disputing and persuading the things concerning the kingdom of God.

9 But when divers were hardened, and believed not, but spoke evil of that way before the multitude, he departed from them, and separated the disciples, disputing daily in the school of one Tyrannus.

10 And this continued by the space of two years; so that all they which dwelled in Asia heard the word of the Lord Jesus, both Jews and Greeks.

11 And God worked special miracles by the hands of Paul:

12 So that from his body were brought to the sick handkerchiefs or aprons, and the diseases departed from them, and the evil spirits went out of them.

13 Then certain of the vagabond Jews, exorcists, took on them to call over them which had evil spirits the name of the LORD Jesus, saying, We adjure you by Jesus whom Paul preaches.

SPEAKING IN TONGUES AND PROPHECY

God used Paul in Ephesus to teach the people about the Holy Spirit. One way God speaks is through tongues and prophecy. Some teach that tongues and prophecy have ceased. Be like a Berean and do your own study. (Acts 19:6)

14 And there were seven sons of one Sceva, a Jew, and chief of the priests, which did so.

15 And the evil spirit answered and said, Jesus I know, and Paul I know; but who are you?

16 And the man in whom the evil spirit was leaped on them, and overcame them, and prevailed against them, so that they fled out of that house naked and wounded.

17 And this was known to all the Jews and Greeks also dwelling at Ephesus; and fear fell on them all, and the name of the Lord Jesus was magnified.

18 And many that believed came, and confessed, and showed their deeds.

19 Many of them also which used curious arts brought their books together, and burned them before all men: and they counted the price of them, and found it fifty thousand pieces of silver.

20 So mightily grew the word of God and prevailed.

21 After these things were ended, Paul purposed in the spirit, when he had passed through Macedonia and Achaia, to go to Jerusalem, saying, After I have been there, I must also see Rome.

22 So he sent into Macedonia two of them that ministered to him, Timotheus and Erastus; but he himself stayed in Asia for a season.

23 And the same time there arose no small stir about that way.

24 For a certain man named Demetrius, a silversmith, which made silver shrines for Diana, brought no small gain to the craftsmen;

DAY 19

⚫	**PURPLE**	Is used when God is speaking directly in the first person.
⚫	**GREEN**	Is used when a passage is talking about God speaking.
⚫	**GOLD**	Is used when God is speaking through non-verbal communication.
⚫	**BROWN**	Is used when Man is speaking on God's behalf in the Third Person.
⚫	**BLUE**	Is used for Angels speaking on God's behalf or a vision or a dream.
✝	**RED**	These are the Words of Jesus.

25 Whom he called together with the workmen of like occupation, and said, Sirs, you know that by this craft we have our wealth.

26 Moreover you see and hear, that not alone at Ephesus, but almost throughout all Asia, this Paul has persuaded and turned away much people, saying that they be no gods, which are made with hands:

27 So that not only this our craft is in danger to be set at nothing; but also that the temple of the great goddess Diana should be despised, and her magnificence should be destroyed, whom all Asia and the world worships.

28 And when they heard these sayings, they were full of wrath, and cried out, saying, Great is Diana of the Ephesians.

29 And the whole city was filled with confusion: and having caught Gaius and Aristarchus, men of Macedonia, Paul's companions in travel, they rushed with one accord into the theatre.

30 And when Paul would have entered in to the people, the disciples suffered him not.

31 And certain of the chief of Asia, which were his friends, sent to him, desiring him that he would not adventure himself into the theatre.

32 Some therefore cried one thing, and some another: for the assembly was confused: and the more part knew not why they were come together.

33 And they drew Alexander out of the multitude, the Jews putting him forward. And Alexander beckoned with the hand, and would have made his defense to the people.

34 But when they knew that he was a Jew, all with one voice about the space of two hours cried out, Great is Diana of the Ephesians.

35 And when the town cleark had appeased the people, he said, You men of Ephesus, what man is there that knows not how that the city of the Ephesians is a worshipper of the great goddess Diana, and of the image which fell down from Jupiter?

SPECIAL MIRACLES

Most believers would be content with ordinary miracles. Paul here experiences special miracles where even handkerchiefs and aprons could be taken from him and put on the sick and they would be healed and set free. (Acts 19:11)

36 Seeing then that these things cannot be spoken against, you ought to be quiet, and to do nothing rashly.

37 For you have brought here these men, which are neither robbers of churches, nor yet blasphemers of your goddess.

38 Why if Demetrius, and the craftsmen which are with him, have a matter against any man, the law is open, and there are deputies: let them accuse one another.

39 But if you inquire anything concerning other matters, it shall be determined in a lawful assembly.

40 For we are in danger to be called in question for this day's uproar, there being no cause whereby we may give an account of this concourse.

41 And when he had thus spoken, he dismissed the assembly.

PERSONAL NOTES

_____

_____

_____

_____

_____

_____

_____

_____

_____

_____

_____

_____

DAY 19   DAILY LESSON

SOME THINGS TO PONDER

1. What did the believers do when Paul laid his hands upon them and prayed for them to receive the Holy Spirit?
   _____
   _____
   _____

2. What were the special miracles Paul was a part of and why might it have been necessary for God to do something like this? Could God do this again? Explain. _____
   _____
   _____

3. What happened when the sons of a religious leader tried to imitate Paul? Why do you think they failed?
   _____
   _____

4. What caused the word of God to prevail in Ephesus as is mentioned in verse 20? _____
   _____
   _____

LEARNING TO HEAR HIM - DAY 19 – OTHER VOICES.

Jesus said in John 10:4, "…the sheep follow him, for they know his voice. 5 And a stranger will they not follow, but will flee from him, for they know not the voice of strangers."

Have you ever heard your dad's voice in your mind when he wasn't there? Maybe you were faced with a decision and you recollected what Dad might say and it was almost like you could hear his voice? What about your mother—ever heard in your head, "Pick up those socks?" And Mom is a thousand miles away. Well, most people answer affirmatively to those questions.

Some people are very aware of the voices in their heads. I wasn't aware of voices for most of my life. I remember, though, once battling with a decision and with hearing God's will. It was a choice that would take me away from home for about three weeks when I had three small children and a lovely wife who had too much on her hands. I also was running a ministry that demanded my time and attention.

I could hear my kids begging me not to go. I could hear my wife's animated voice saying, "What? You want to go off and travel around the world and have fun while I watch these kids? I don't think so!" (This is not what she said, but it is what I imagined in my head she would say.) Then I heard my board of directors when I asked if the ministry would fund this trip. None of the voices in my head was affirmative. It was only the still small voice of God that was saying yes, and to be honest, at that time His voice was not the loudest in my head. Sometimes we fear man more than God.

DAY 19

DAILY LESSON

WEEK 3 | LESSON 19

LEARNING TO HEAR HIM - DAY 19 – OTHER VOICES.

What people are going to think or say can be more important than what is God telling me. For me it took the proverbial two-by-four upside the head to start listening to God and not fearing men.

Some people hear voices, and they are demonic voices, telling them to hurt themselves and others. Many times those voices are accusatory, threatening and yet so familiar and real that people are paralyzed by listening to the enemy's voice.

One woman who I was ministering to had condemning religious spirits that tormented her. When she would want to listen to God, all she heard was condemnation and how she was no good. When I called out the spirit, she went deaf momentarily. The voices in her head got louder. Then I took authority over the spirits and she could hear me and began to hear God instead of the lies of spirits that were totally familiar to her. She had believed that it was God speaking to her in the past, condemning her, and had never realized the enemy was masquerading before her.

Throughout the Bible there were false prophets and people who were influenced by lying spirits. Spirits can masquerade as the Holy Spirit and deceive people. The occult operates by demonic powers and sometimes those same spirits come into the church without people being aware. Sometimes people are deceived by listening to false spirits.

There is nowhere in scripture that we are warned to not even try listening to God because we might listen to the wrong spirit. Don't use such faulty logic and throw the baby out with the bath water.

We don't have to be fooled by the deceiver. We can learn to discern. We need to get to know God and His Word to help us discern when we are listening to evil spirits or our own imagination of what others might say.

Don't let this scare you. Let this truth make you humble and wise as you listen. Hearing God must come from humility. We can all be deceived at some time so it is okay to seek confirmation and test every spirit.

MAKING IT PERSONAL:

1. Are you aware of hearing different voices in your head? Mom's voice, Dad's, your spouse? Explain. _____
   _____
   _____

2. Are you ever aware of hearing suggestions by the enemy in your spirit, your mind? What does it sound like to you? _____
   _____

3. Can you tell the difference between God's voice and the other voices in your head? Ever find it difficult? Explain. _____
   _____

TIME TO LISTEN

Write in the space below whatever God may be speaking to you. Don't censor it as you write. If a song comes to mind pay attention to the words and write them. If scripture, write down the reference or the verse, if random thoughts write them. If you see images in your mind write them. Afterward ask God for discernment as to what each thing means.

_____

_____

_____

_____

_____

_____

_____

_____

_____

_____

_____

_____

_____

_____

_____

_____

_____

_____

_____

_____

_____

_____

_____

DAY 20

	PURPLE	Is used when God is speaking directly in the first person.
	GREEN	Is used when a passage is talking about God speaking.
	GOLD	Is used when God is speaking through non-verbal communication.
	BROWN	Is used when Man is speaking on God's behalf in the Third Person.
	BLUE	Is used for Angels speaking on God's behalf or a vision or a dream.
	RED	These are the Words of Jesus.

ACTS: CHAPTER 20

1 And after the uproar was ceased, Paul called to him the disciples, and embraced them, and departed for to go into Macedonia.

2 And when he had gone over those parts, and had given them much exhortation, he came into Greece,

3 And there stayed three months. And when the Jews laid wait for him, as he was about to sail into Syria, he purposed to return through Macedonia.

4 And there accompanied him into Asia Sopater of Berea; and of the Thessalonians, Aristarchus and Secundus; and Gaius of Derbe, and Timotheus; and of Asia, Tychicus and Trophimus.

5 These going before tarried for us at Troas.

6 And we sailed away from Philippi after the days of unleavened bread, and came to them to Troas in five days; where we stayed seven days.

7 And on the first day of the week, when the disciples came together to break bread, Paul preached to them, ready to depart on the morrow; and continued his speech until midnight.

8 And there were many lights in the upper chamber, where they were gathered together.

9 And there sat in a window a certain young man named Eutychus, being fallen into a deep sleep: and as Paul was long preaching, he sunk down with sleep, and fell down from the third loft, and was taken up dead.

10 And Paul went down, and fell on him, and embracing him said, Trouble not yourselves; for his life is in him.

11 When he therefore was come up again, and had broken bread, and eaten, and talked a long while, even till break of day, so he departed.

12 And they brought the young man alive, and were not a little comforted.

13 And we went before to ship, and sailed to Assos, there intending to take in Paul: for so had he appointed, minding himself to go afoot.

HOLY SPIRIT DIRECTS PAUL AND WARNS HIM

It seems that Paul was compelled in his human spirit to go to Jerusalem, even though, the Holy Spirit was warning him that he would suffer there. Was Paul's spirit in tune with the Holy Spirit or contrary? (Acts 20:22-23)

14 And when he met with us at Assos, we took him in, and came to Mitylene.

15 And we sailed there, and came the next day over against Chios; and the next day we arrived at Samos, and tarried at Trogyllium; and the next day we came to Miletus.

16 For Paul had determined to sail by Ephesus, because he would not spend the time in Asia: for he hurried, if it were possible for him, to be at Jerusalem the day of Pentecost.

17 And from Miletus he sent to Ephesus, and called the elders of the church.

18 And when they were come to him, he said to them, You know, from the first day that I came into Asia, after what manner I have been with you at all seasons,

19 Serving the LORD with all humility of mind, and with many tears, and temptations, which befell me by the lying in wait of the Jews:

20 And how I kept back nothing that was profitable to you, but have showed you, and have taught you publicly, and from house to house,

21 Testifying both to the Jews, and also to the Greeks, repentance toward God, and faith toward our Lord Jesus Christ.

22 And now, behold, I go bound in the spirit to Jerusalem, not knowing the things that shall befall me there:

23 Save that the Holy Ghost witnesses in every city, saying that bonds and afflictions abide me.

	PURPLE	Is used when God is speaking directly in the first person.
	GREEN	Is used when a passage is talking about God speaking.
	GOLD	Is used when God is speaking through non-verbal communication.
	BROWN	Is used when Man is speaking on God's behalf in the Third Person.
	BLUE	Is used for Angels speaking on God's behalf or a vision or a dream.
	RED	These are the Words of Jesus.

24 But none of these things move me, neither count I my life dear to myself, so that I might finish my course with joy, and the ministry, which I have received of the Lord Jesus, to testify the gospel of the grace of God.

25 And now, behold, I know that you all, among whom I have gone preaching the kingdom of God, shall see my face no more.

26 Why I take you to record this day, that I am pure from the blood of all men.

27 For I have not shunned to declare to you all the counsel of God.

28 Take heed therefore to yourselves, and to all the flock, over the which the Holy Ghost has made you overseers, to feed the church of God, which he has purchased with his own blood.

29 For I know this, that after my departing shall grievous wolves enter in among you, not sparing the flock.

30 Also of your own selves shall men arise, speaking perverse things, to draw away disciples after them.

31 Therefore watch, and remember, that by the space of three years I ceased not to warn everyone night and day with tears.

32 And now, brothers, I commend you to God, and to the word of his grace, which is able to build you up, and to give you an inheritance among all them which are sanctified.

33 I have coveted no man's silver, or gold, or apparel.

34 Yes, you yourselves know, that these hands have ministered to my necessities, and to them that were with me.

35 I have showed you all things, how that so laboring you ought to support the weak, and to remember the words of the Lord Jesus, how he said, It is more blessed to give than to receive.

36 And when he had thus spoken, he kneeled down, and prayed with them all.

37 And they all wept sore, and fell on Paul's neck, and kissed him,

38 Sorrowing most of all for the words which he spoke, that they should see his face no more. And they accompanied him to the ship.

PERSONAL NOTES

_____
_____
_____
_____
_____
_____
_____
_____
_____
_____
_____
_____
_____
_____
_____
_____
_____
_____
_____
_____
_____
_____
_____
_____
_____
_____
_____
_____
_____

DAILY LESSON

SOME THINGS TO PONDER

1. What miracle encouraged the believers in Troas as much as any of Paul's preaching did? _____
   _____
   _____
   _____

2. What was the Holy Spirit saying about Paul going to Jerusalem and what was Paul's spirit saying? _____
   _____
   _____

3. Do you think that Paul was ignoring what the Holy Spirit was saying? Was it Paul's own decision to go or God's? (reread vs. 23-24) _____
   _____
   _____

4. Who was directing the things that Paul was preaching? _____
   _____
   _____

LEARNING TO HEAR HIM - DAY 20 – A WORD FROM THE MAN OF GOD

Many people want a Word from the Lord from a man of God. It can put someone who is considered prophetic on the spot. I love sharing with people what God speaks to me. However, I'd rather take the time to teach people how to listen to the Lord themselves. For some it is their gift to speak prophetic words, like Agabus here in Acts.

I love listening to what the Lord has to say to a person, but it is more beneficial for them if they don't have to wait for someone else to hear from God. That is part of our Lord's promise if we have the Holy Spirit. He will speak to us and He will lead us.

People also like other people who have encouraging, and positive words for them. What if what God has to say is not positive and encouraging but has to do with God's anger or displeasure? Some don't believe God could be like that, and serve a God that they have imagined who is always happy and encouraging.

Many of the gifts of God involve God speaking words through members of His body for other people. The gifts of teaching, prophesy, exhortation, words of knowledge, words of wisdom, interpretation of tongues, and evangelism especially operate in this way. We are all to be listening to God and sharing with His body what He is speaking to all of us.

We need to watch out for the tendency today to exalt men and positions and have celebrities. God wants His sheep to know His voice, not be chasing the next "man of God" for a "word."

DAY 20   DAILY LESSON

WEEK 3 | LESSON 20

MAKING IT PERSONAL:

1. Have you or others you have known become fixated on getting a word from God from a "man of God" in an unhealthy way? Explain. _____

_____

_____

2. Are you still open to God speaking through others and hearing from God for you? Explain. _____

_____

_____

3. Describe what you believe is a healthy way to view hearing God speak through others? _____

_____

TIME TO LISTEN

Write in the space below whatever God may be speaking to you. Don't censor it as you write. If a song comes to mind pay attention to the words and write them. If scripture, write down the reference or the verse, if random thoughts write them. If you see images in your mind write them. Afterward ask God for discernment as to what each thing means. _____

_____

_____

_____

_____

_____

_____

_____

_____

_____

_____

_____

_____

DAY 21

WEEK 3 | LESSON 21

	PURPLE	Is used when God is speaking directly in the first person.
	GREEN	Is used when a passage is talking about God speaking.
	GOLD	Is used when God is speaking through non-verbal communication.
	BROWN	Is used when Man is speaking on God's behalf in the Third Person.
	BLUE	Is used for Angels speaking on God's behalf or a vision or a dream.
	RED	These are the Words of Jesus.

ACTS: CHAPTER 21

1 And it came to pass, that after we were gotten from them, and had launched, we came with a straight course to Coos, and the day following to Rhodes, and from there to Patara:

2 And finding a ship sailing over to Phenicia, we went aboard, and set forth.

3 Now when we had discovered Cyprus, we left it on the left hand, and sailed into Syria, and landed at Tyre: for there the ship was to unlade her burden.

4 And finding disciples, we tarried there seven days: who said to Paul through the Spirit, that he should not go up to Jerusalem.

5 And when we had accomplished those days, we departed and went our way; and they all brought us on our way, with wives and children, till we were out of the city: and we kneeled down on the shore, and prayed.

6 And when we had taken our leave one of another, we took ship; and they returned home again.

7 And when we had finished our course from Tyre, we came to Ptolemais, and saluted the brothers, and stayed with them one day.

8 And the next day we that were of Paul's company departed, and came to Caesarea: and we entered into the house of Philip the evangelist, which was one of the seven; and stayed with him.

9 And the same man had four daughters, virgins, which did prophesy.

10 And as we tarried there many days, there came down from Judaea a certain prophet, named Agabus.

11 And when he was come to us, he took Paul's girdle, and bound his own hands and feet, and said, Thus said the Holy Ghost, So shall the Jews at Jerusalem bind the man that owns this girdle, and shall deliver him into the hands of the Gentiles.

12 And when we heard these things, both we, and they of that place, sought him not to go up to Jerusalem.

MULTIPLE WARNINGS

It seems like everyone was warning Paul about going to Jerusalem. There was the witness of the Holy Spirit, disciples in Tyre, the prophet Agabus, and finally there was a direct vision from God. (Acts 21:4, 9-11)

13 Then Paul answered, What mean you to weep and to break my heart? For I am ready not to be bound only, but also to die at Jerusalem for the name of the Lord Jesus.

14 And when he would not be persuaded, we ceased, saying, The will of the Lord be done.

15 And after those days we took up our carriages, and went up to Jerusalem.

PERSONAL NOTES

_____
_____
_____
_____
_____
_____
_____
_____
_____
_____
_____
_____
_____
_____
_____
_____

16 There went with us also certain of the disciples of Caesarea, and brought with them one Mnason of Cyprus, an old disciple, with whom we should lodge.

17 And when we were come to Jerusalem, the brothers received us gladly.

18 And the day following Paul went in with us to James; and all the elders were present.

19 And when he had saluted them, he declared particularly what things God had worked among the Gentiles by his ministry.

20 And when they heard it, they glorified the Lord, and said to him, You see, brother, how many thousands of Jews there are which believe; and they are all zealous of the law:

21 And they are informed of you, that you teach all the Jews which are among the Gentiles to forsake Moses, saying that they ought not to circumcise their children, neither to walk after the customs.

22 What is it therefore? The multitude must needs come together: for they will hear that you are come.

23 Do therefore this that we say to you: We have four men which have a vow on them;

24 Them take, and purify yourself with them, and be at charges with them, that they may shave their heads: and all may know that those things, whereof they were informed concerning you, are nothing; but that you yourself also walk orderly, and keep the law.

25 As touching the Gentiles which believe, we have written and concluded that they observe no such thing, save only that they keep themselves from things offered to idols, and from blood, and from strangled, and from fornication.

26 Then Paul took the men, and the next day purifying himself with them entered into the temple, to signify the accomplishment of the days of purification, until that an offering should be offered for everyone of them.

27 And when the seven days were almost ended, the Jews which were of Asia, when they saw him in the temple, stirred up all the people, and laid hands on him,

28 Crying out, Men of Israel, help: This is the man, that teaches all men everywhere against the people, and the law, and this place: and further brought Greeks also into the temple, and has polluted this holy place.

29 (For they had seen before with him in the city Trophimus an Ephesian, whom they supposed that Paul had brought into the temple.)

30 And all the city was moved, and the people ran together: and they took Paul, and drew him out of the temple: and immediately the doors were shut.

31 And as they went about to kill him, tidings came to the chief captain of the band, that all Jerusalem was in an uproar.

32 Who immediately took soldiers and centurions, and ran down to them: and when they saw the chief captain and the soldiers, they left beating of Paul.

33 Then the chief captain came near, and took him, and commanded him to be bound with two chains; and demanded who he was, and what he had done.

34 And some cried one thing, some another, among the multitude: and when he could not know the certainty for the tumult, he commanded him to be carried into the castle.

35 And when he came on the stairs, so it was, that he was borne of the soldiers for the violence of the people.

36 For the multitude of the people followed after, crying, Away with him.

37 And as Paul was to be led into the castle, he said to the chief captain, May I speak to you? Who said, Can you speak Greek?

38 Are not you that Egyptian, which before these days made an uproar, and led out into the wilderness four thousand men that were murderers?

39 But Paul said, I am a man which am a Jew of Tarsus, a city in Cilicia, a citizen of no mean city: and, I beseech you, suffer me to speak to the people.

40 And when he had given him license, Paul stood on the stairs, and beckoned with the hand to the people. And when there was made a great silence, he spoke to them in the Hebrew tongue, saying...

(continued on Day 22)

PURPLE	Is used when God is speaking directly in the first person.
GREEN	Is used when a passage is talking about God speaking.
GOLD	Is used when God is speaking through non-verbal communication.
BROWN	Is used when Man is speaking on God's behalf in the Third Person.
BLUE	Is used for Angels speaking on God's behalf or a vision or a dream.
RED	These are the Words of Jesus.

SOME THINGS TO PONDER

1. Whose spirit in verse 4 is compelling Paul not to go to Jerusalem? _____

_____

_____

2. In the book of Acts, how did the church respond to someone prophesying? How did Paul respond?

_____

_____

3. Paul was being accused of speaking against God's Word and the Law? Was that true? Why would he be accused of that? _____

_____

_____

LEARNING TO HEAR HIM - DAY 21 – OUR OWN IMAGINATION

Another hindrance to hearing God is our own imagination. Our own thoughts, desires and motives can affect what we believe we are hearing.

I have heard people say God told them everyone present was supposed to join them in some business venture (multi-level marketing). They waxed eloquent about how God wanted all of us to be financially secure and this was the means God had chosen to that end. I'm not saying God has never said something like this. However, it was easy for me to know where this came from, but not for the person who thought they were hearing from God. They really thought they had heard God. Those thoughts had been in their head and were the controlling thoughts. They couldn't hear God because they were consumed with developing their downline and becoming rich.

DAY 21

DAILY LESSON

WEEK 3 | LESSON 21

LEARNING TO HEAR HIM - DAY 21 – OUR OWN IMAGINATION

As we've discussed, our own imagination can get in the way of us hearing God. Look at what God spoke in Jeremiah 11:6: "Then the LORD said unto me, 'Proclaim all these words in the cities of Judah and in the streets of Jerusalem, saying, "Hear ye the words of this covenant and do them. 7 For I earnestly protested unto your fathers in the day that I brought them up out of the land of Egypt, even unto this day, rising early and protesting, saying, 'Obey My voice.' 8 Yet they obeyed not, nor inclined their ear, but walked everyone in the imagination of their evil heart. Therefore I will bring upon them all the words of this covenant, which I commanded them to do, but they did them not."

Everyone walked in the imagination of their evil heart. Are we any different today? The same was said of the false prophets—that they prophesied out of their own imagination. People were prophesying that peace and prosperity were coming, waxing eloquent and becoming popular while Jeremiah gave the true word of the Lord.

I remember one time when I was at a church and the pastor and a friend of mine put me on the spot. I was new in hearing God's voice and they called people forward to hear a "Word from God from the prophet." I was scared spitless. I had never had to hear God on command for hundreds of different people. For the first three people I operated totally out of my own imagination and I felt foolish and powerless but was trying to do a great job faking it. Then I felt convicted. I told the Lord, "I can't do this." The next person came forward and I said to the Lord, "I will not say another word unless you speak." What happened next was amazing and wonderful. God took over. At the end I was left wondering how often people fake it. How often do people speak things for God because it is expected of them in certain churches, and they have become good at saying fanciful and imaginative things?

Ask God as you listen to set you free from your own imagination. This can be so hard for some. It is usually rooted in pride and hard-heartedness. Very religious people can be bound in this. It is very dangerous to believe you are hearing from God if your are operating in your own imagination. If you are discerning, it is easy to spot, but a lot of people can be fooled. Pray that God sets you free from your pride and any vain imagination as you listen to Him.

MAKING IT PERSONAL:

1. Have you been in a place where people are expected to hear from God and you suspected or discerned that it was not God but their own imaginations? If so, how did you feel? _____

   _____

2. Have you found yourself ever allowing your own imagination to make you think that God was leading you but it was not God? Explain. _____

   _____

   _____

   _____

DAY 21 DAILY LESSON

WEEK 3 | LESSON 21

TIME TO LISTEN

Write in the space below whatever God may be speaking to you. Don't censor it as you write. If a song comes to mind pay attention to the words and write them. If scripture, write down the reference or the verse, if random thoughts write them. If you see images in your mind write them. Afterward ask God for discernment as to what each thing means.

_____

_____

_____

_____

_____

_____

_____

_____

_____

_____

_____

_____

_____

_____

_____

_____

_____

_____

_____

_____

_____

GOD SPEAKS

LEARN HOW TO HEAR GOD

A JOURNEY THROUGH THE BOOK OF ACTS

SECTION

4

WEEK 4 | LESSONS 22-28
STUDY GUIDE

GOD SPEAKS
LEARN HOW TO HEAR GOD
A JOURNEY THROUGH THE BOOK OF ACTS

WEEK 4 | LESSON 22-28
UNIQUE WAYS GOD SPEAKS

God uses some amazing ways to speak to His people, don't you think? Have you paid attention as you have read the chapters each day as to how many times God gave someone a vision or a dream? Have you noticed how many times angels or God Himself showed up in some manner? Take a quick look at Appendix 1 and see all the various ways that God spoke to people throughout the book of Acts.

Acts 2: 15 "For these are not drunken, as you suppose, seeing it is but the third hour of the day. 16 But this is that which was spoken by the prophet Joel; 17 And it shall come to pass in the last days, said God, I will pour out of my Spirit on all flesh: and your sons and your daughters shall prophesy, and your young men shall see visions, and your old men shall dream dreams: 18 And on my servants and on my handmaidens I will pour out in those days of my Spirit; and they shall prophesy: 19 And I will show wonders in heaven above, and signs in the earth beneath; blood, and fire, and vapor of smoke: 20 The sun shall be turned into darkness, and the moon into blood, before the great and notable day of the Lord come: 21 And it shall come to pass, that whoever shall call on the name of the Lord shall be saved."

If this happened in Acts and it is prophesied that this will happen in the last days, are we not in the last days? God is getting His bride ready, and part of that task is equipping His bride to know His voice as opposed to the voice of our enemy.

VISIONS OR IMAGINATIONS
I remember when I first started thinking that I might be able to learn to hear God. I would be still and listen and pay no attention to the images that were dancing around in my head. Now, I have learned to pay attention to those images and scenes and words

that come to my mind. The images used to drive me crazy. Now, I realize God is speaking to me in visions. In my experience most people will see visions when they listen to God once they learn how to listen. Most tell me they never paid attention to those images before.

It is also possible to imagine things in our own minds and create images. God warned us numerous times in scripture from speaking out of our own imagination. He rebuked false prophets for speaking from their own imagination. When God is speaking to us the images come to us and we are not in control of anything except taking the time to listen and pay attention. When we imagine, our will is engaged and we can form the images in our minds.

Sometimes people use their own imaginations when they read and interpret scripture to make it say what they want. They use their imagination to prophesy and preach. Just because the false exists doesn't mean it is all false or even that most is false. In scripture most prophesy is real and the warnings against false dreams and visions are real but they are not many. In other words, we don't have to fear visions or dreams. We just need to be sure that the source isn't our soul but the Spirit of God. Sometimes God makes it clear that He is the one communicating with us by sending a messenger.

HEAVENLY VISITORS
There are so many unique visitations in the book of Acts as well as throughout the entire Bible. What an exciting and wonderful way for God to communicate with us!

My favorite example of this in scripture is in Daniel Chapters 9-10. Gabriel shows up several times and three times calls Daniel a man of high esteem. I have a holy envy, if there is such a thing. Can you imagine Gabriel telling you that you are held in high esteem in heaven? What an amazing quiet time. What about Paul's encounter on the road to Damascus or the night God visited Paul in Acts 24:11? Those were incredible as well.

One thing that I had never noticed was that many of the visits by angels were in visions or in dreams. I believe that a vision is when God peels back the veil that covers our eyes so that we can see what is already right around us in the spiritual realm. The Bible teaches us that angels are real, they have jobs, they bring messages, they minister, they deliver food sometimes and so much more. Some angels fell and they have through time interacted with mankind. The study of angels is very worthwhile, though I would caution you to study it from scripture and not the internet. The New Age movement has produced a lot about angels, and that is definitely not a healthy source of information.

Ask any group of people if they have ever seen an angel and you will be amazed. Many people have seen angels at one time or another. The first time I saw one was in the first vision that I was aware was from God. I was lying on my living room floor and though my eyes were closed I saw an angel at my feet putting a sheet over me. Someone else in the room said, "An angel is putting a mantle on me." That was pretty freaky to me since the man was describing what I had just seen. I didn't realize it was a mantle until the man said it. I was saying nothing and giving no clues as to what I was seeing. How did he know?

Angels were not the only heavenly visitors in Acts. Jesus and God himself visited people numerous times. Sometimes God showed up in visions and a few times in person. If God has been doing that all throughout history, why would He stop now? If God is so personable, why would He stop communing with people when the scriptures became canonized, as some suggest? That would mark a significant change in God's character and practice as opposed to any time in history.

I used to have a hard time when someone would say something like "God spoke to me" or "Jesus came to me in a vision". I would immediately tune the person out and think he was a flake. That changed after my own personal encounters. I don't seek to build my theology on my experience but once something has happened to you, it is hard to deny it. You can't fake it. You know it is real. Then when you look at scripture, the blinders are gone and you read that what you experienced is normal Christianity. It is one of the ways God works. Then when you hear the same lies you used to teach or believe being told to someone else, it is so grievous.

MIRACLE, SIGNS AND WONDERS

God has communicated all throughout history through signs, wonders and miracles. Yes, miracles can be faked. Pharaoh's magicians faked some plagues like those that God had sent. But they couldn't keep up with God. The fact that magicians could fake plagues does not lessen the reality that God was doing these signs and wonders to show the world that He alone was the true God. It worked. The nations all around became fearful of messing with God's people. God is doing the same thing in Acts through the miracles, signs and wonders. He is displaying His power and drawing people to Himself. He wants to do the same thing today through His church if we would only believe and come to understand who we are and the power that is ours.

Ever wonder what the difference is between signs, wonders and miracles? Well, here are some working definitions for you to consider. Miracles are supernatural acts that are beyond human ability. Healing the sick, raising the dead, causing blindness in a sorcerer were all miraculous acts. Signs are visual displays, usually supernatural but not always, that exhibit some aspect of God's character or nature. Wonders are like signs but take place in the heavenly realm, like the mighty rushing wind from heaven in Acts 2. Signs and wonders are normally mentioned together and normally accompany one another.

To be honest I used to avoid these terms because they elicited images in my mind of televangelist asking for money.

As you are honest with God's Word, meaning you let it say what it says, you find out that signs, wonders and miracles are found all throughout scripture and they are one way that God has always communicated. Begin to pay attention to the things that happen around you and listen to God's voice. He may use the incidents of your normal day to speak to you by a sign, wonder or miracle.

HOLY SPIRIT

One primary way that God speaks is through His Holy Spirit communing with our spirit. This is the subject of our second lesson, but I did want to mention it again. It is vital for us to realize that we have a spirit and we have the Holy Spirit. We need to be led by God's Spirit, not our flesh and not our soul. Learn to listen to the Holy Spirit. Since the Holy Spirit was poured out, God has been communicating with us via the Holy Spirit, who is God. Jesus taught that the Holy Spirit would lead us into all truth and teach us all things. He taught that the Holy Spirit would bring things to our remembrance (John 15-16). Paul charges us with a command to be filled with the Holy Spirit in Ephesians 5:18. He is telling us to be constantly be filled with the Holy Spirit. Being filled is not a one-time experience. We must be constantly filling our tanks with the Holy Spirit and the power from heaven.

We must learn to listen to what the Holy Spirit is saying to us. There are not descriptions for us of anyone seeing the Holy Spirit or of what His voice sounds like. It was more than likely not an audible voice. Spirit communes with spirit differently.

CONCLUSION

God does not fit in anyone's nice little box. He communicates in so many different and unique ways. It seems like no two encounters in the Bible are alike. There are similarities, but God does not have a cookie cutter way of communicating. He is the Creator, and creativity is part of who God is. Open up to some new ways of God speaking to you. Be sure that what you hear lines up with scripture. In 1 Samuel 28:7-19, King Saul had disobeyed God, and God's Spirit had left Saul. In his desperation to hear God, Saul went to a witch in Endor, which was clearly forbidden in God's Word. In this rare case God obliged Saul and sent Samuel from the dead to communicate with Saul. The message that God spoke through Samuel was that this act of disobedience was going to cost Saul his life and the life of his son and that the Philistines would defeat Israel the next day. There are ways that we should never try to get revelation. Occult practices are not the way to hear from God.

DAY 22

	PURPLE	Is used when God is speaking directly in the first person.
	GREEN	Is used when a passage is talking about God speaking.
	GOLD	Is used when God is speaking through non-verbal communication.
	BROWN	Is used when Man is speaking on God's behalf in the Third Person.
	BLUE	Is used for Angels speaking on God's behalf or a vision or a dream.
	RED	These are the Words of Jesus.

ACTS: CHAPTER 22

1 Men, brothers, and fathers, hear you my defense which I make now to you.

2 (And when they heard that he spoke in the Hebrew tongue to them, they kept the more silence: and he said,)

3 I am truly a man which am a Jew, born in Tarsus, a city in Cilicia, yet brought up in this city at the feet of Gamaliel, and taught according to the perfect manner of the law of the fathers, and was zealous toward God, as you all are this day.

4 And I persecuted this way to the death, binding and delivering into prisons both men and women.

5 As also the high priest does bear me witness, and all the estate of the elders: from whom also I received letters to the brothers, and went to Damascus, to bring them which were there bound to Jerusalem, for to be punished.

6 And it came to pass, that, as I made my journey, and was come near to Damascus about noon, suddenly there shone from heaven a great light round about me.

7 And I fell to the ground, and heard a voice saying to me, Saul, Saul, why persecute you me?

8 And I answered, Who are you, Lord? And he said to me, I am Jesus of Nazareth, whom you persecute.

9 And they that were with me saw indeed the light, and were afraid; but they heard not the voice of him that spoke to me.

10 And I said, What shall I do, LORD? And the Lord said to me, Arise, and go into Damascus; and there it shall be told you of all things which are appointed for you to do.

11 And when I could not see for the glory of that light, being led by the hand of them that were with me, I came into Damascus.

12 And one Ananias, a devout man according to the law, having a good report of all the Jews which dwelled there,

13 Came to me, and stood, and said to me, Brother

THE POWER OF TESTIMONY

Paul recounts his story as often as he can find opportunity. What an amazing and dramatic story it is. Your story cannot be disputed. No one could deny what Paul had experienced. It was compelling to see the transformation from persecutor to evangelist. (Acts 22:6-19)

Saul, receive your sight. And the same hour I looked up on him.

14 And he said, The God of our fathers has chosen you, that you should know his will, and see that Just One, and should hear the voice of his mouth.

15 For you shall be his witness to all men of what you have seen and heard.

16 And now why tarry you? arise, and be baptized, and wash away your sins, calling on the name of the Lord.

17 And it came to pass, that, when I was come again to Jerusalem, even while I prayed in the temple, I was in a trance;

18 And saw him saying to me, Make haste, and get you quickly out of Jerusalem: for they will not receive your testimony concerning me.

19 And I said, Lord, they know that I imprisoned and beat in every synagogue them that believed on you:

20 And when the blood of your martyr Stephen was shed, I also was standing by, and consenting to his death, and kept the raiment of them that slew him.

21 And he said to me, Depart: for I will send you far hence to the Gentiles.

22 And they gave him audience to this word, and then lifted up their voices, and said, Away with such a fellow from the earth: for it is not fit that he should live.

23 And as they cried out, and cast off their clothes, and threw dust into the air,

24 The chief captain commanded him to be brought

	PURPLE	Is used when God is speaking directly in the first person.
	GREEN	Is used when a passage is talking about God speaking.
	GOLD	Is used when God is speaking through non-verbal communication.
	BROWN	Is used when Man is speaking on God's behalf in the Third Person.
	BLUE	Is used for Angels speaking on God's behalf or a vision or a dream.
	RED	These are the Words of Jesus.

into the castle, and bade that he should be examined by scourging; that he might know why they cried so against him.

25 And as they bound him with thongs, Paul said to the centurion that stood by, Is it lawful for you to whip a man that is a Roman, and uncondemned?

26 When the centurion heard that, he went and told the chief captain, saying, Take heed what you do: for this man is a Roman.

27 Then the chief captain came, and said to him, Tell me, are you a Roman? He said, Yes.

28 And the chief captain answered, With a great sum obtained I this freedom. And Paul said, But I was free born.

29 Then straightway they departed from him which should have examined him: and the chief captain also was afraid, after he knew that he was a Roman, and because he had bound him.

30 On the morrow, because he would have known the certainty why he was accused of the Jews, he loosed him from his bands, and commanded the chief priests and all their council to appear, and brought Paul down, and set him before them.

PERSONAL NOTES

DAY 22   DAILY LESSON

WEEK 4 | LESSON 22

SOME THINGS TO PONDER

1. What was the foundation of Paul's defense before the people of Jerusalem? His experience/scripture? Why?

_____

_____

2. As Paul shares his testimony, how many instances does He include of God speaking to him or another person?

_____

_____

3. How did the people respond to Paul's testimony? Why? Who were they rejecting? _____

_____

_____

4. How did Paul receive his call to minister to the gentiles? Was it confirmed by another? Explain: _____

_____

_____

LEARNING TO HEAR HIM - DAY 22– GOD SHOWS OFF

Normally when we use the words "show off" we can mean them in a derogatory manner. But when God shows off it is brilliant. When you see lightning flashing across the sky, stand amongst the Swiss Alps or on the rim of the Grand Canyon, you can't help but believe God loves to show off. Throughout history, part of how God revealed himself and showed mankind who He is and what He was like is through signs, wonders and miracles.

Growing up in church, we would hardly use words like miracles, signs, and wonders. In Hebrews 2:3-4 we read, "3 How shall we escape, if we neglect so great salvation; which at the first began to be spoken by the Lord, and was confirmed unto us by them that heard him; 4 God also bearing them witness, both with signs and wonders, and with divers miracles, and gifts of the Holy Ghost, according to his own will?" We see that God was communicating with us about salvation through signs, wonders and different kinds of miracles.

Often God speaks by actions. Nonverbal communication is a very vital form of communication. The old adage, "Actions speak louder than words," is so true when it comes to God.

The frequency with which the Lord did miracles in the Bible is impressive. It is easy to understand what a miracle is. A miracle is anything that demonstrates God's supernatural power to perform mighty acts. It comes from the Greek word dunamis.

Signs are supernatural events or occurrences that are visual in nature. The distinction is the emphasis on a miraculous occurrence that is seen. The word wonders is found in the Bible twenty-four times and always accompanies the word signs. The main difference is that wonders happen in heaven and signs take place on earth.

GOD SPEAKS   121   SECTION 4: WEEK 4 | LESSONS 22-28

DAY 22
DAILY LESSON
WEEK 4 | LESSON 22

LEARNING TO HEAR HIM - DAY 22 – GOD SHOWS OFF

In Acts 2 there is a verse that weaves each of these different words together in one moment and one event.

Acts 2: 2 "And suddenly there came a sound from heaven as of a rushing mighty wind, and it filled all the house where they were sitting. 3 And there appeared unto them cloven tongues like as of fire, and it sat upon each of them. 4 And they were all filled with the Holy Ghost, and began to speak with other tongues, as the Spirit gave them utterance."

It starts with a wonder of a sound that came from heaven like a rushing mighty wind that filled all the house. Then a sign followed, in the form of tongues of fire that sat on each of the people gathered. And finally they began to miraculously speak in other languages as the Holy Spirit gave them utterance.

At Jesus' baptism we hear a voice from heaven, which was a wonder, then a dove alights on Jesus, which was a sign, and soon after that Jesus began to do miracles. The apostles did signs, wonders and miracles. Even Stephen was not an apostle but a deacon, and he was noted as one who did wonders and miracles among the people.

In Jesus' day the disciples tried to stop someone who was doing miracles because they were mistakenly believing that it was only they who were supposed to do miracles. Jesus rebuked them. Then, in Luke 10 Jesus sent out seventy-two others to do miracles of healing. We know nothing about those seventy-two except that God called them little children and that it brought Him great joy when they went out and did miracles. Jesus even mentioned seeing a wonder of Satan falling like lightning from heaven.

God still reveals himself today through signs, wonders and miracles.

MAKING IT PERSONAL:

1. How many signs, wonders and miracles can you think of throughout the Bible? _____
   _____

2. Did you grow up believing in and hearing about signs, wonders and miracles? _____
   _____

3. What are some motives that could affect your ability to hear God clearly? _____
   _____

DAY 22

DAILY LESSON

WEEK 4 | LESSON 22

TIME TO LISTEN

Write in the space below whatever God may be speaking to you. Don't censor it as you write. If a song comes to mind pay attention to the words and write them. If scripture, write down the reference or the verse, if random thoughts write them. If you see images in your mind write them. Afterward ask God for discernment as to what each thing means.

	PURPLE	Is used when God is speaking directly in the first person.
	GREEN	Is used when a passage is talking about God speaking.
	GOLD	Is used when God is speaking through non-verbal communication.
	BROWN	Is used when Man is speaking on God's behalf in the Third Person.
	BLUE	Is used for Angels speaking on God's behalf or a vision or a dream.
	RED	These are the Words of Jesus.

ACTS: CHAPTER 23

1 And Paul, earnestly beholding the council, said, Men and brethren, I have lived in all good conscience before God until this day.

2 And the high priest Ananias commanded them that stood by him to smite him on the mouth.

3 Then said Paul unto him, God shall smite thee, thou whited wall: for sittest thou to judge me after the law, and commandest me to be smitten contrary to the law?

4 And they that stood by said, Revilest thou God's high priest?

5 Then said Paul, I wist not, brethren, that he was the high priest: for it is written, Thou shalt not speak evil of the ruler of thy people.

6 But when Paul perceived that the one part were Sadducees, and the other Pharisees, he cried out in the council, Men and brethren, I am a Pharisee, the son of a Pharisee: of the hope and resurrection of the dead I am called in question.

7 And when he had so said, there arose a dissension between the Pharisees and the Sadducees: and the multitude was divided.

8 For the Sadducees say that there is no resurrection, neither angel, nor spirit: but the Pharisees confess both.

9 And there arose a great cry: and the scribes that were of the Pharisees' part arose, and strove, saying, We find no evil in this man: but if a spirit or an angel hath spoken to him, let us not fight against God.

10 And when there arose a great dissension, the chief captain, fearing lest Paul should have been pulled in pieces of them, commanded the soldiers to go down, and to take him by force from among them, and to bring him into the castle.

11 And the night following the Lord stood by him, and said, Be of good cheer, Paul: for as thou hast testified of me in Jerusalem, so must thou bear witness also at Rome.

HAS GOD STOPPED TALKING?

Some have concluded that the later chapters of Acts show that God was starting to no longer do miracles and give dreams and visions. The premise is that now that we have the Bible we don't need any more revelations from God than a Bible and preaching of the Word. Those who say this often pride themselves on being true to God's Word. God's Word reveals a God who never stops talking. Don't be fooled. God is talking to you.

12 And when it was day, certain of the Jews banded together, and bound themselves under a curse, saying that they would neither eat nor drink till they had killed Paul.

13 And they were more than forty which had made this conspiracy.

14 And they came to the chief priests and elders, and said, We have bound ourselves under a great curse, that we will eat nothing until we have slain Paul.

15 Now therefore ye with the council signify to the chief captain that he bring him down unto you tomorrow, as though ye would enquire something more perfectly concerning him: and we, or ever he come near, are ready to kill him.

16 And when Paul's sister's son heard of their lying in wait, he went and entered into the castle, and told Paul.

17 Then Paul called one of the centurions unto him, and said, Bring this young man unto the chief captain: for he hath a certain thing to tell him.

18 So he took him, and brought him to the chief captain, and said, Paul the prisoner called me unto him, and prayed me to bring this young man unto thee, who hath something to say unto thee.

19 Then the chief captain took him by the hand, and went with him aside privately, and asked him, What is that thou hast to tell me?

	PURPLE	Is used when God is speaking directly in the first person.
	GREEN	Is used when a passage is talking about God speaking.
	GOLD	Is used when God is speaking through non-verbal communication.
	BROWN	Is used when Man is speaking on God's behalf in the Third Person.
	BLUE	Is used for Angels speaking on God's behalf or a vision or a dream.
	RED	These are the Words of Jesus.

20 And he said, The Jews have agreed to desire thee that thou wouldest bring down Paul tomorrow into the council, as though they would enquire somewhat of him more perfectly.

21 But do not thou yield unto them: for there lie in wait for him of them more than forty men, which have bound themselves with an oath, that they will neither eat nor drink till they have killed him: and now are they ready, looking for a promise from thee.

22 So the chief captain then let the young man depart, and charged him, See thou tell no man that thou hast shewed these things to me.

23 And he called unto him two centurions, saying, Make ready two hundred soldiers to go to Caesarea, and horsemen threescore and ten, and spearmen two hundred, at the third hour of the night;

24 And provide them beasts, that they may set Paul on, and bring him safe unto Felix the governor.

25 And he wrote a letter after this manner:

26 Claudius Lysias unto the most excellent governor Felix sendeth greeting.

27 This man was taken of the Jews, and should have been killed of them: then came I with an army, and rescued him, having understood that he was a Roman.

28 And when I would have known the cause wherefore they accused him, I brought him forth into their council:

29 Whom I perceived to be accused of questions of their law, but to have nothing laid to his charge worthy of death or of bonds.

30 And when it was told me how that the Jews laid wait for the man, I sent straightway to thee, and gave commandment to his accusers also to say before thee what they had against him. Farewell.

31 Then the soldiers, as it was commanded them, took Paul, and brought him by night to Antipatris.

32 On the morrow they left the horsemen to go with him, and returned to the castle:

33 Who, when they came to Caesarea, and delivered the epistle to the governor, presented Paul also before him.

34 And when the governor had read the letter, he asked of what province he was. And when he understood that he was of Cilicia;

35 I will hear thee, said he, when thine accusers are also come. And he commanded him to be kept in Herod's judgment hall.

PERSONAL NOTES

SOME THINGS TO PONDER

1. What did Paul experience the night before he went before the judge? How would you like to experience that?

_____

_____

2. How was Paul warned of the threat that was on his life? Was there anything supernatural about this? Explain.

_____

_____

3. Did God deliver Paul from the hands of his accusers or was it natural circumstances? _____

_____

_____

LEARNING TO HEAR HIM - DAY 23 – THE WORD OF THE LORD WAS RARE

There was a time in Israel's history when "…the Word of the Lord was rare…" (1 Samuel 3:1). The people were not listening to God. The same thing happens today. When people stop listening, then the Word of the Lord is rare. I have often wondered about that passage.

Why did God stop talking for a period of time? I believe that the answer lies in Judges 17, which tells us about this time in history. Judges 17:6 says, "In those days there was no king in Israel, but every man did that which was right in his own eyes." The question shouldn't be why God stopped speaking but rather why the people stopped listening.

I saw this illustrated yesterday in my own house. My son, Andrew, had asked God to speak to him in dreams, and he began to have a dream almost every night. Some held meaning for other friends or family but some hit home. In one, God was telling him that football had become an idol. Well, yesterday, Mom (my wife Dawn) was sharing about two dreams that both spoke to the fact that Andrew was joking around and hurting people's feelings. Andrew, half serious and half joking, said that he was ready for the dreams to stop.

If we listen to God, God starts meddling in our business. He can speak great words of comfort and He can bring correction. Both are vital but we all prefer the comfort to the correction.

We have to watch out for making God like us. What do I mean by that? Many times we can think that what we believe about a matter is the voice of God and then we are the god in our lives. How is listening to God different than listening to our own thoughts? That is an excellent question.

DAY 23
WEEK 4 | LESSON 23

DAILY LESSON

SOME THINGS TO PONDER

Our own imagination can mimic the voice of God. That is why we have to walk with great humility when we think we are hearing from God.

1. Have we let our own desires cloud our perspective on what we are hearing? _____

_____

2. Have we let our emotions get in the way? _____

3. Are we intentionally shutting out the voice of God because we don't want to hear what He has to say? _____

4. Have we created a god in our own mind that is nothing like the God of the Bible but who we think we can handle better? _____

_____

_____

These are some of the real dangers we need to watch out for, but they can't keep us from listening. Ask God to silence your own will when you are truly seeking to hear Him in regard to something. Ask Him to calm your emotions on the subject. Don't shut out His voice because you are afraid what He is going to say.

The key is to get to know the God of the Bible so well that you trust Him with your entire life. He is trustworthy.

MAKING IT PERSONAL:

1. As you have been listening to God have you found God dealing with specific things in your life that He wanted to change? How did that feel? _____

_____

_____

2. Have you experienced seasons in your life where you didn't hear from God for a long time? Explain: ___

_____

_____

3. Have you ever intentionally shut out God's voice? Why? _____

_____

_____

DAY 23

DAILY LESSON

WEEK 4 | LESSON 23

TIME TO LISTEN

Write in the space below whatever God may be speaking to you. Don't censor it as you write. If a song comes to mind pay attention to the words and write them. If scripture, write down the reference or the verse, if random thoughts write them. If you see images in your mind write them. Afterward ask God for discernment as to what each thing means.

_____

_____

_____

_____

_____

_____

_____

_____

_____

_____

_____

ACTS: CHAPTER 24

1 And after five days Ananias the high priest descended with the elders, and with a certain orator named Tertullus, who informed the governor against Paul.

2 And when he was called forth, Tertullus began to accuse him, saying, Seeing that by you we enjoy great quietness, and that very worthy deeds are done to this nation by your providence,

3 We accept it always, and in all places, most noble Felix, with all thankfulness.

4 Notwithstanding, that I be not further tedious to you, I pray you that you would hear us of your clemency a few words.

5 For we have found this man a pestilent fellow, and a mover of sedition among all the Jews throughout the world, and a ringleader of the sect of the Nazarenes:

6 Who also has gone about to profane the temple: whom we took, and would have judged according to our law.

7 But the chief captain Lysias came on us, and with great violence took him away out of our hands,

8 Commanding his accusers to come to you: by examining of whom yourself may take knowledge of all these things, whereof we accuse him.

9 And the Jews also assented, saying that these things were so.

10 Then Paul, after that the governor had beckoned to him to speak, answered, For as much as I know that you have been of many years a judge to this nation, I do the more cheerfully answer for myself:

11 Because that you may understand, that there are yet but twelve days since I went up to Jerusalem for to worship.

12 And they neither found me in the temple disputing with any man, neither raising up the people, neither in the synagogues, nor in the city:

13 Neither can they prove the things whereof they now accuse me.

14 But this I confess to you, that after the way which they call heresy, so worship I the God of my fathers, believing all things which are written in the law and in the prophets:

15 And have hope toward God, which they themselves also allow, that there shall be a resurrection of the dead, both of the just and unjust.

SEASONS OF SILENCE

In our lives, as throughout history, it can seem at times like God is silent. Often we don't know how to hear God so we are not hearing what He is saying. Other times we just are not listening. Sometimes the Lord wants us to press in to Him. We've grown distant and don't realize it. Sometimes the Lord wants us to be patient. The answer is coming.

16 And herein do I exercise myself, to have always a conscience void to offense toward God, and toward men.

17 Now after many years I came to bring alms to my nation, and offerings.

18 Whereupon certain Jews from Asia found me purified in the temple, neither with multitude, nor with tumult.

19 Who ought to have been here before you, and object, if they had ought against me.

20 Or else let these same here say, if they have found any evil doing in me, while I stood before the council,

21 Except it be for this one voice, that I cried standing among them, Touching the resurrection of the dead I am called in question by you this day.

22 And when Felix heard these things, having more perfect knowledge of that way, he deferred them, and said, When Lysias the chief captain shall come down, I will know the uttermost of your matter.

23 And he commanded a centurion to keep Paul, and to let him have liberty, and that he should forbid none of his acquaintance to minister or come to him.

24 And after certain days, when Felix came with his wife Drusilla, which was a Jewess, he sent for Paul, and heard him concerning the faith in Christ.

25 And as he reasoned of righteousness, temperance, and judgment to come, Felix trembled, and answered, Go your way for this time; when I have a convenient season, I will call for you.

26 He hoped also that money should have been given him of Paul, that he might lose him: why he sent for him the oftener, and communed with him.

27 But after two years Porcius Festus came into Felix' room: and Felix, willing to show the Jews a pleasure, left Paul bound.

SOME THINGS TO PONDER

1. This is the first chapter in Acts where there isn't a reference to God speaking in some way. Does that mean God stopped communicating during this season? What are other options? _____

_____

_____

2. If Paul knew that this type of imprisonment was coming, what purpose did it serve for him to go to Jerusalem?

_____

_____

3. Paul used to be the hero of the religious leaders of his day, but now they are out to destroy him and kill him. What would incite and inspire such extreme reaction? Who is ultimately behind this? Explain: _____

_____

_____

LEARNING TO HEAR HIM - DAY 24 – FALSE REVELATIONS

False dreams, visions, prophecies, even angels, lying signs and wonders and false christs. All of these have been a part of reality since man has been around. We are promised that in the last days this will increase. We are also promised in Joel 2 and in Acts 2 that in the last days we will see an increase in dreams and visions.

It is vital to realize that both exist, the real and the false, the genuine and the counterfeit. It is sad to see those believers and churches who totally exclude the possibility of God communicating today in any of these ways because they have seen the false. It is just as sad to see the believers and churches that don't operate in discernment and who believe every prophet, every dreamer, and therefore every charlatan.

The way to spot a counterfeit is to study the real thing and spend as much time with the real thing as possible. The more familiar you are with what the scriptures say about God speaking and the more familiar you become with His voice the more you will be able to discern when someone is speaking a lie.

Sometimes people can walk in a mixture. They hear from God and then they let their own flesh get in the way. That was what Balaam was wrestling with. He would hear God and yet he was motivated by greed. Sometimes people want to promote themselves, so their prophetic word can include self-promotion. Sometimes a person's biases or wounds can affect their ability to hear clearly or cause them to add their own interpretation or other content to what God speaks to them.

It is wise to be discerning as we hear others share what they believe God is speaking to them. It is also imperative to ask the Lord to search our hearts regarding anything we would share when we believe God is speaking to us, especially when it pertains to another person.

DAY 24

DAILY LESSON

MAKING IT PERSONAL:

1. Have you ever seen false prophets, dreams that weren't from God or people claiming to be a messiah or to have a special revelation? Explain. _____
_____
_____

2. What is a wise response when you see something that is false? _____
_____
_____

3. Because some people have and will continue to speak false words from God of every kind, should we not allow people to listen to God, speak on behalf of God, or share a dream or vision? Why do you agree or disagree? ____
_____
_____

TIME TO LISTEN

Write in the space below whatever God may be speaking to you. Don't censor it as you write. If a song comes to mind pay attention to the words and write them. If scripture, write down the reference or the verse, if random thoughts write them. If you see images in your mind write them. Afterward ask God for discernment as to what each thing means.

_____
_____
_____
_____
_____
_____
_____
_____
_____
_____
_____
_____

	PURPLE	Is used when God is speaking directly in the first person.
	GREEN	Is used when a passage is talking about God speaking.
	GOLD	Is used when God is speaking through non-verbal communication.
	BROWN	Is used when Man is speaking on God's behalf in the Third Person.
	BLUE	Is used for Angels speaking on God's behalf or a vision or a dream.
	RED	These are the Words of Jesus.

ACTS: CHAPTER 25

1 Now when Festus was come into the province, after three days he ascended from Caesarea to Jerusalem.

2 Then the high priest and the chief of the Jews informed him against Paul, and sought him,

3 And desired favor against him, that he would send for him to Jerusalem, laying wait in the way to kill him.

4 But Festus answered, that Paul should be kept at Caesarea, and that he himself would depart shortly thither.

5 Let them therefore, said he, which among you are able, go down with me, and accuse this man, if there be any wickedness in him.

6 And when he had tarried among them more than ten days, he went down to Caesarea; and the next day sitting on the judgment seat commanded Paul to be brought.

7 And when he was come, the Jews which came down from Jerusalem stood round about, and laid many and grievous complaints against Paul, which they could not prove.

8 While he answered for himself, Neither against the law of the Jews, neither against the temple, nor yet against Caesar, have I offended anything at all.

9 But Festus, willing to do the Jews a pleasure, answered Paul, and said, Will you go up to Jerusalem, and there be judged of these things before me?

10 Then said Paul, I stand at Caesar's judgment seat, where I ought to be judged: to the Jews have I done no wrong, as you very well know.

11 For if I be an offender, or have committed anything worthy of death, I refuse not to die: but if there be none of these things whereof these accuse me, no man may deliver me to them. I appeal to Caesar.

12 Then Festus, when he had conferred with the council, answered, Have you appealed to Caesar? to Caesar shall you go.

13 And after certain days king Agrippa and Bernice came to Caesarea to salute Festus.

14 And when they had been there many days, Festus declared Paul's cause to the king, saying, There is a certain man left in bonds by Felix:

15 About whom, when I was at Jerusalem, the chief priests and the elders of the Jews informed me, desiring to have judgment against him.

16 To whom I answered, It is not the manner of the Romans to deliver any man to die, before that he which is accused have the accusers face to face, and have license to answer for himself concerning the crime laid against him.

18 Against whom when the accusers stood up, they brought none accusation of such things as I supposed:

19 But had certain questions against him of their own superstition, and of one Jesus, which was dead, whom Paul affirmed to be alive.

20 And because I doubted of such manner of questions, I asked him whether he would go to Jerusalem, and there be judged of these matters.

21 But when Paul had appealed to be reserved to the hearing of Augustus, I commanded him to be kept till I might send him to Caesar.

22 Then Agrippa said to Festus, I would also hear the man myself. Tomorrow, said he, you shall hear him.

23 And on the morrow, when Agrippa was come, and Bernice, with great pomp, and was entered into the place of hearing, with the chief captains, and principal men of the city, at Festus' commandment Paul was brought forth.

24 And Festus said, King Agrippa, and all men which are here present with us, you see this man, about whom all the multitude of the Jews have dealt with me, both at Jerusalem, and also here, crying that he ought not to live any longer.

25 But when I found that he had committed nothing worthy of death, and that he himself has appealed to Augustus, I have determined to send him.

26 Of whom I have no certain thing to write to my lord. Why I have brought him forth before you, and specially before you, O king Agrippa, that, after examination had, I might have somewhat to write.

27 For it seems to me unreasonable to send a prisoner, and not with to signify the crimes laid against him.

	PURPLE	Is used when God is speaking directly in the first person.
	GREEN	Is used when a passage is talking about God speaking.
	GOLD	Is used when God is speaking through non-verbal communication.
	BROWN	Is used when Man is speaking on God's behalf in the Third Person.
	BLUE	Is used for Angels speaking on God's behalf or a vision or a dream.
	RED	These are the Words of Jesus.

SOME THINGS TO PONDER

1. Why do you think that Paul appealed to Caesar's judgment? _____

_____

_____

2. What does Festus think about the charges that have been brought by the Jews against Paul? _____

_____

_____

3. If there are no miracles, dreams or visions described in this chapter, does that mean they have ceased? Explain why you believe it does or doesn't. _____

_____

_____

LEARNING TO HEAR HIM - DAY 25 – LISTENING TO OTHERS

Throughout the Bible God would speak to people and tell them to share what He had spoken with others. Noah heard from God for himself and his family. Moses and Aaron and sometimes the elders would hear from God for the entire nation of Jorad. Throughout Acts and the New Testament, God would speak to and through His people in a myriad of ways. We see angels bringing messages in Acts 1, and in Acts 2 all those who gathered in the upper room were speaking to a multitude of people in their own languages.

As you trace this idea through Acts you see people having visions that contained messages for themselves and for others. You see people encountering angels who brought them messages as well as words to share with others. You see prophets bringing the Word of the Lord to God's people and many more examples.

As a ministry Operation Light Force offers personal ministry to people in need of physical, mental and emotional healing as well as healing for marriages. One of the things that has begun to mark our time with people is that we normally start with taking time to be still and listen to see what God has to say to the person and to us as ministers.

As we do take this time and listen, people learn to hear God's voice. Most haven't taken time to listen either ever or in a long time. Every time God has spoken, God's wisdom and the power of what He says far transcends our best ministry. Almost every time we share what God is speaking, people want it written down. They testify that what God said is what sustained them, what ministered to them the most.

Many times people assume that they are being led by God without taking time to listen. Joshua assumed he was the leader and could make decisions on his own when the men from Gibeon came to make a treaty with him (Joshua 9). He caused trouble for centuries in Israel by not taking time to listen to God about that decision.

God wants to speak to us every day about all types of decisions. There is nothing more valuable than listening to God's voice and doing what He asks of us. It is especially important when we are in positions of authority since what we do has a significant impact upon the lives of others around us. Therefore God would sometimes give people messages for those in authority. This was often a dangerous role.

Jeremiah was thrown into prison for the words God had sent him to share with the king. Many were killed throughout history for the words God had spoken to them for others. It is not always well received when we share with others what God speaks to and through His people. I find that God often speaks lovingly and affectionately to His people. He also often brings words of correction and rebuke, but always in love.

Nothing can be more life-giving to others than hearing from God, even if it is through another person bringing that message. On the other hand, few things can be more destructive than religious judgments and some of the atrocities that riddle history which were done in the name of God. Be careful but not afraid as you listen to God and you believe he has spoken something to you that could benefit another person.

DAY 25　DAILY LESSON

WEEK 4 | LESSON 25

MAKING IT PERSONAL:

1. Describe a time God sent someone to you to speak a message to you from Him. _____
_____
_____

2. Describe a time when God spoke something to you for someone else. _____
_____
_____

3. Have you had a time when someone came to you with a message from God but you knew it wasn't
really from God? Describe it. _____
_____

TIME TO LISTEN

Write in the space below whatever God may be speaking to you. Don't censor it as you write. If a song comes to mind pay attention to the words and write them. If scripture, write down the reference or the verse, if random thoughts write them. If you see images in your mind write them. Afterward ask God for discernment as to what each thing means.

_____
_____
_____
_____
_____
_____
_____
_____
_____
_____
_____
_____
_____
_____
_____
_____

PURPLE	Is used when God is speaking directly in the first person.
GREEN	Is used when a passage is talking about God speaking.
GOLD	Is used when God is speaking through non-verbal communication.
BROWN	Is used when Man is speaking on God's behalf in the Third Person.
BLUE	Is used for Angels speaking on God's behalf or a vision or a dream.
RED	These are the Words of Jesus.

ACTS: CHAPTER 26

1 Then Agrippa said to Paul, You are permitted to speak for yourself. Then Paul stretched forth the hand, and answered for himself:

2 I think myself happy, king Agrippa, because I shall answer for myself this day before you touching all the things whereof I am accused of the Jews:

3 Especially because I know you to be expert in all customs and questions which are among the Jews: why I beseech you to hear me patiently.

4 My manner of life from my youth, which was at the first among my own nation at Jerusalem, know all the Jews;

5 Which knew me from the beginning, if they would testify, that after the most strait sect of our religion I lived a Pharisee.

6 And now I stand and am judged for the hope of the promise made of God, to our fathers:

7 To which promise our twelve tribes, instantly serving God day and night, hope to come. For which hope's sake, king Agrippa, I am accused of the Jews.

8 Why should it be thought a thing incredible with you, that God should raise the dead?

9 I truly thought with myself, that I ought to do many things contrary to the name of Jesus of Nazareth.

10 Which thing I also did in Jerusalem: and many of the saints did I shut up in prison, having received authority from the chief priests; and when they were put to death, I gave my voice against them.

11 And I punished them oft in every synagogue, and compelled them to blaspheme; and being exceedingly mad against them, I persecuted them even to strange cities.

12 Whereupon as I went to Damascus with authority and commission from the chief priests,

13 At midday, O king, I saw in the way a light from heaven, above the brightness of the sun, shining round about me and them which journeyed with me.

OBEDIENT TO THE VISION

Some people want to give different value to various means of God speaking. Paul here set his entire life direction around a heavenly vision. It is important to be wise. If someone gives you a "Word from God" that you should marry a certain person, wait on the Lord for confirmation. (Acts 26:19)

14 And when we were all fallen to the earth, I heard a voice speaking to me, and saying in the Hebrew tongue, Saul, Saul, why persecute you me? it is hard for you to kick against the pricks.

15 And I said, Who are you, Lord? And he said, I am Jesus whom you persecute.

16 But rise, and stand on your feet: for I have appeared to you for this purpose, to make you a minister and a witness both of these things which you have seen, and of those things in the which I will appear to you;

17 Delivering you from the people, and from the Gentiles, to whom now I send you,

18 To open their eyes, and to turn them from darkness to light, and from the power of Satan to God, that they may receive forgiveness of sins, and inheritance among them which are sanctified by faith that is in me.

19 Whereupon, O king Agrippa, I was not disobedient to the heavenly vision:

20 But showed first to them of Damascus, and at Jerusalem, and throughout all the coasts of Judaea, and then to the Gentiles, that they should repent and turn to God, and do works meet for repentance.

21 For these causes the Jews caught me in the temple, and went about to kill me.

22 Having therefore obtained help of God, I continue to this day, witnessing both to small and great, saying none other things than those which the prophets and Moses

did say should come:

23 That Christ should suffer, and that he should be the first that should rise from the dead, and should show light to the people, and to the Gentiles.

24 And as he thus spoke for himself, Festus said with a loud voice, Paul, you are beside yourself; much learning does make you mad.

25 But he said, I am not mad, most noble Festus; but speak forth the words of truth and soberness.

26 For the king knows of these things, before whom also I speak freely: for I am persuaded that none of these things are hidden from him; for this thing was not done in a corner.

27 King Agrippa, believe you the prophets? I know that you believe.

28 Then Agrippa said to Paul, Almost you persuade me to be a Christian.

29 And Paul said, I would to God, that not only you, but also all that hear me this day, were both almost, and altogether such as I am, except these bonds.

30 And when he had thus spoken, the king rose up, and the governor, and Bernice, and they that sat with them:

31 And when they were gone aside, they talked between themselves, saying, This man does nothing worthy of death or of bonds.

32 Then said Agrippa to Festus, This man might have been set at liberty, if he had not appealed to Caesar.

PERSONAL NOTES

DAY 26
DAILY LESSON
WEEK 4 | LESSON 26

SOME THINGS TO PONDER

1. Does Paul's testimony ever get old? Why do you think He shares it again and again? _____

_____

2. In verse 19, Paul focuses his obedience on following what form of revelation? Why is that significant to point out?

_____

3. Paul said to King Agrippa that he wished that Agrippa would be like himself except for the chains. What does that tell us about how Paul was faring as a prisoner? _____

_____

LEARNING TO HEAR HIM - DAY 26 – RELIGION VS. RELATIONSHIP

One of the hardest realities to separate from the voice of God is all of our traditional religious garbage. For many who have been steeped in church and the rules of our religious upbringing it is hard to separate that from real relationship with God. Our traditions too often triumph over truth. We believe our religious rules are the truth and can miss real truth. This was the problem of the Scribes, Pharisees, Sadducees, and teachers of the law had in Jesus' day.

For example, someone who is tattooed all over comes to you or to your small group for prayer, and you believe tattoos are of the devil (not a time for debate on this subject, okay?). It will be hard for you to hear God or to possibly even listen to the person. What might be screaming in your ears if you have had such contempt for tattoos? It might be pure judgment, but I know many people who actually have a lot of compassion but their total judgment is clouded by the outward appearance.

Years ago I served in a church that was full of unwritten rules: "Hats off in God's house," "Suits required," "Cut your hair, you hippie," "If you are not from here, you are not from here," "etc." One day a guy I had been witnessing to came in with shorts on and I could see the elders gathered in the back with scowls on their faces discussing whether to ask him to leave. I offered them my resignation if they did anything besides welcome him. No wonder people wouldn't stay. They were not fleeing God but the religious garbage. One day a teen came to me and said, "I love Jesus and I love you but I am NEVER coming back to church again." I couldn't blame him, though I knew he needed a fellowship of believers.

Recently one woman, while listening to God, felt such condemnation. I immediately knew that it was not God but a familiar voice that, in her mind, impersonated God but wasn't God at all. She began to recognize the difference between the condemnation that permeated her family, her church, and her entire region of the country and God's voice. When God brings correction it is without condemnation. God rebukes out of love. The enemy rebukes out of condemnation.

Religious condemnation says, "You are a bad person." God's rebuke lovingly communicates that, "If you continue in your sin, there will be consequences that I don't want you to face." Yes, God rebukes, and He chastises, but always out of love. I feel His love and guidance and care when the Lord corrects me.

Ask God to reveal to you all the religious beliefs that you may have believed were from God but were man-made. Ask God to set you free from those things so that you can hear Him better.

DAY 26   DAILY LESSON

MAKING IT PERSONAL:

1. Are you from a background that is full of religious traditions? _____
   _____

2. Do you tend to experience condemnation when listening to God or in your own mind and heart in regard
   to your faith or any area of your life? Explain: _____
   _____

3. What are some religious rules you have been a part of that are not found in God's Word? _____
   _____

TIME TO LISTEN

Write in the space below whatever God may be speaking to you. Don't censor it as you write. If a song comes to mind
pay attention to the words and write them. If scripture, write down the reference or the verse, if random thoughts write
them. If you see images in your mind write them. Afterward ask God for discernment as to what each thing means

_____

_____

_____

_____

_____

_____

_____

_____

_____

_____

_____

_____

_____

_____

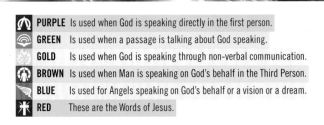

ACTS: CHAPTER 27

1 And when it was determined that we should sail into Italy, they delivered Paul and certain other prisoners to one named Julius, a centurion of Augustus' band.

2 And entering into a ship of Adramyttium, we launched, meaning to sail by the coasts of Asia; one Aristarchus, a Macedonian of Thessalonica, being with us.

3 And the next day we touched at Sidon. And Julius courteously entreated Paul, and gave him liberty to go to his friends to refresh himself.

4 And when we had launched from there, we sailed under Cyprus, because the winds were contrary.

5 And when we had sailed over the sea of Cilicia and Pamphylia, we came to Myra, a city of Lycia.

6 And there the centurion found a ship of Alexandria sailing into Italy; and he put us therein.

7 And when we had sailed slowly many days, and scarce were come over against Cnidus, the wind not suffering us, we sailed under Crete, over against Salmone;

8 And, hardly passing it, came to a place which is called The fair havens; near whereunto was the city of Lasea.

9 Now when much time was spent, and when sailing was now dangerous, because the fast was now already past, Paul admonished them,

10 And said to them, Sirs, I perceive that this voyage will be with hurt and much damage, not only of the lading and ship, but also of our lives.

11 Nevertheless the centurion believed the master and the owner of the ship, more than those things which were spoken by Paul.

12 And because the haven was not commodious to winter in, the more part advised to depart there also, if by any means they might attain to Phenice, and there to winter; which is an haven of Crete, and lies toward the south west and north west.

13 And when the south wind blew softly, supposing that they had obtained their purpose, loosing there, they sailed close by Crete.

THE FINAL WORD

Paul had many people warn him about going to Jerusalem. Some wept in Ephesus, telling him not to go. Finally God spoke in a vision what Paul already knew. God had a great purpose for Paul going to Jerusalem. (Acts 27:22-24)

14 But not long after, there arose against it a tempestuous wind, called Euroclydon.

15 And when the ship was caught, and could not bear up into the wind, we let her drive.

16 And running under a certain island which is called Clauda, we had much work to come by the boat:

17 Which when they had taken up, they used helps, undergirding the ship; and, fearing lest they should fall into the quicksands, struck sail, and so were driven.

18 And we being exceedingly tossed with a tempest, the next day they lightened the ship;

19 And the third day we cast out with our own hands the tackling of the ship.

20 And when neither sun nor stars in many days appeared, and no small tempest lay on us, all hope that we should be saved was then taken away.

21 But after long abstinence Paul stood forth in the middle of them, and said, Sirs, you should have listened to me, and not have loosed from Crete, and to have gained this harm and loss.

22 And now I exhort you to be of good cheer: for there shall be no loss of any man's life among you, but of the ship.

23 For there stood by me this night the angel of God, whose I am, and whom I serve,

24 Saying, Fear not, Paul; you must be brought before Caesar: and, see, God has given you all them that sail with you.

25 Why, sirs, be of good cheer: for I believe God, that it shall be even as it was told me.

	PURPLE	Is used when God is speaking directly in the first person.
	GREEN	Is used when a passage is talking about God speaking.
	GOLD	Is used when God is speaking through non-verbal communication.
	BROWN	Is used when Man is speaking on God's behalf in the Third Person.
	BLUE	Is used for Angels speaking on God's behalf or a vision or a dream.
	RED	These are the Words of Jesus.

26 However, we must be cast on a certain island.

27 But when the fourteenth night was come, as we were driven up and down in Adria, about midnight the shipmen deemed that they drew near to some country;

28 And sounded, and found it twenty fathoms: and when they had gone a little further, they sounded again, and found it fifteen fathoms.

29 Then fearing lest we should have fallen on rocks, they cast four anchors out of the stern, and wished for the day.

30 And as the shipmen were about to flee out of the ship, when they had let down the boat into the sea, under color as though they would have cast anchors out of the bow,

31 Paul said to the centurion and to the soldiers, Except these abide in the ship, you cannot be saved.

32 Then the soldiers cut off the ropes of the boat, and let her fall off.

33 And while the day was coming on, Paul sought them all to take meat, saying, This day is the fourteenth day that you have tarried and continued fasting, having taken nothing.

34 Why I pray you to take some meat: for this is for your health: for there shall not an hair fall from the head of any of you.

35 And when he had thus spoken, he took bread, and gave thanks to God in presence of them all: and when he had broken it, he began to eat.

36 Then were they all of good cheer, and they also took some meat.

37 And we were in all in the ship two hundred three score and sixteen souls.

38 And when they had eaten enough, they lightened the ship, and cast out the wheat into the sea

39 And when it was day, they knew not the land: but they discovered a certain creek with a shore, into the which they were minded, if it were possible, to thrust in the ship.

PROPHETIC KNOWLEDGE

In two verses Paul speaks authoritatively to those who are shipwrecked with him in verses Acts 27:22, 34. How does he know this? God spoke it to him and Paul had a vision. When God reveals something to us it gives us confidence that others around us don't have.

40 And when they had taken up the anchors, they committed themselves to the sea, and loosed the rudder bands, and hoisted up the mainsail to the wind, and made toward shore.

41 And falling into a place where two seas met, they ran the ship aground; and the forepart stuck fast, and remained unmovable, but the hinder part was broken with the violence of the waves.

42 And the soldiers' counsel was to kill the prisoners, lest any of them should swim out, and escape.

43 But the centurion, willing to save Paul, kept them from their purpose; and commanded that they which could swim should cast themselves first into the sea, and get to land:

44 And the rest, some on boards, and some on broken pieces of the ship. And so it came to pass, that they escaped all safe to land.

PERSONAL NOTES

_____

_____

_____

_____

_____

_____

_____

_____

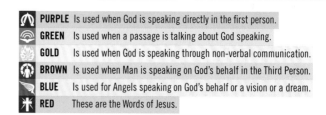

PURPLE Is used when God is speaking directly in the first person.
GREEN   Is used when a passage is talking about God speaking.
GOLD   Is used when God is speaking through non-verbal communication.
BROWN   Is used when Man is speaking on God's behalf in the Third Person.
BLUE   Is used for Angels speaking on God's behalf or a vision or a dream.
RED   These are the Words of Jesus.

SOME THINGS TO PONDER

1. How did Paul know that no one who was on the ship with him would die? _____

_____

_____

2. How could Paul speak with such authority to these people that everyone could eat and that no one would lose a hair from his head? _____

_____

_____

3. What earlier promise had God made to Paul that also gave him confidence in knowing that he would make it through this ordeal? _____

_____

_____

DAILY LESSON

LEARNING TO HEAR HIM - DAY 27 – SUMMARY

GOD IS STILL TALKING.

God has been communicating throughout history with mankind. He has communicated in many different ways to all kinds of people. He wants to guide us and teach us and speak to us, His children. The problem is not with God's communication, it is with our ears. We need ears to hear what God is saying to us.

GOD TALKS TO ALL KINDS OF PEOPLE.

God doesn't just talk to important people. He talks to servants, boys and girls, kings, pagans and Christians. He talks to the rich and the poor, those who are old and those who are young. He speaks to people in every language and throughout all of history. God loves to communicate, even down to minute details.

GOD TALKS IN MANY DIFFERENT WAYS IN EVERY LANGUAGE.

People in all parts of the world hear God. He comes to them in their dreams, and sends angels in person and in visions. God speaks through prophets, priests, farmers, factory workers, housewives, CEOs and secretaries. He can speak with a voice from heaven, a whisper. He loves to show off and speak through signs and wonders and miracles. He's even spoken through a donkey in Numbers and a fish in Jonah. God even talks to Himself and to nothing during the creation in Genesis.

> He speaks through the sunrise, the forest rain,
>
> The majestic mountains, the valley streams,
>
> The birds in the sky, the trees of the field,
>
> The fish of the sea and even through me.

Oh, that we would learn to hear Him as well as He communicates!

People sometimes get it wrong – but don't give up.

Throughout time, people have thought they heard God and gone forward into all kinds of trouble. There have been false prophets, false visions, false dreams, and lying signs and wonders. We are also told that in the last days they will increase and that we will even have false christs. For some the logic says, since it is fraught with so much falsehood, don't even try to listen to God. That logic, if applied to driving, would abandon vehicles due to the fact that there are accidents, car theft, road rage, drunk drivers, etc. Can I just call it like it is? Unsound logic.

If the Bible said, anywhere not to listen to God, or if He has told us everything we ever needed to hear and wrote it in the Bible, or if God doesn't talk to us anymore in the ways He always has, then burn this book and try me as a heretic. I've spent three years deeply researching this subject biblically and haven't found one passage that says, "God decided it was time to stop communicating". Don't give up. You absolutely can hear Him, and don't be afraid that you might get it wrong.

DAY 27   DAILY LESSON

WEEK 4 | LESSON 27

WE NEED TO LISTEN.

People are not going to hear God if they don't learn how to be still and listen. There is more to listening than being still, but it is a great place to start. It is possible for you to hear God in the midst of noise, chaos, and confusion, but it is much easier to listen when you are still and in a quiet place. You will have to become more aware of your spirit to hear God well. God is spirit and has sent us the Holy Spirit. So much of God's communication is with our spirit that it is vital for us to learn to listen to what is going on in our spirit.

WE NEED WILLING HEARTS.

In order to listen we need to trust God. He is trustworthy. If God is going to speak to us then we must have willing hearts. Trusting God opens us up to receiving whatever God has for us. It opens us up to hearing whatever He has to say. Fear will keep us from listening. The expectation that God has something bad in store for us will keep us from listening.

MAKING IT PERSONAL

1. What has been the greatest challenge for you in learning to hear God's voice as you have journeyed with us through Acts? _____
_____
_____

2. What new way have you discovered that God still speaks? _____
_____
_____

3. What lesson along the way stands out to you in learning to hear God's voice? _____
_____
_____

DAY 27

DAILY LESSON

WEEK 4 | LESSON 27

TIME TO LISTEN

Write in the space below whatever God may be speaking to you. Don't censor it as you write. If a song comes to mind pay attention to the words and write them. If scripture, write down the reference or the verse, if random thoughts write them. If you see images in your mind write them. Afterward ask God for discernment as to what each thing means.

_____

_____

_____

_____

_____

_____

_____

_____

_____

_____

_____

_____

_____

_____

_____

_____

_____

_____

_____

_____

_____

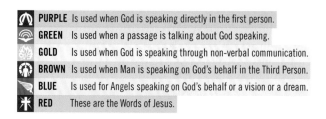

PURPLE	Is used when God is speaking directly in the first person.
GREEN	Is used when a passage is talking about God speaking.
GOLD	Is used when God is speaking through non-verbal communication.
BROWN	Is used when Man is speaking on God's behalf in the Third Person.
BLUE	Is used for Angels speaking on God's behalf or a vision or a dream.
RED	These are the Words of Jesus.

ACTS: CHAPTER 28

1 And when they were escaped, then they knew that the island was called Melita.

2 And the barbarous people showed us no little kindness: for they kindled a fire, and received us everyone, because of the present rain, and because of the cold.

3 And when Paul had gathered a bundle of sticks, and laid them on the fire, there came a viper out of the heat, and fastened on his hand.

4 And when the barbarians saw the venomous beast hang on his hand, they said among themselves, No doubt this man is a murderer, whom, though he has escaped the sea, yet vengeance suffers not to live.

5 And he shook off the beast into the fire, and felt no harm.

6 However, they looked when he should have swollen, or fallen down dead suddenly: but after they had looked a great while, and saw no harm come to him, they changed their minds, and said that he was a god.

7 In the same quarters were possessions of the chief man of the island, whose name was Publius; who received us, and lodged us three days courteously.

8 And it came to pass, that the father of Publius lay sick of a fever and of a bloody flux: to whom Paul entered in, and prayed, and laid his hands on him, and healed him.

9 So when this was done, others also, which had diseases in the island, came, and were healed:

10 Who also honored us with many honors; and when we departed, they laded us with such things as were necessary.

11 And after three months we departed in a ship of Alexandria, which had wintered in the isle, whose sign was Castor and Pollux.

12 And landing at Syracuse, we tarried there three days.

13 And from there we fetched a compass, and came to Rhegium: and after one day the south wind blew, and we came the next day to Puteoli:

14 Where we found brothers, and were desired to tarry with them seven days: and so we went toward Rome.

15 And from there, when the brothers heard of us, they came to meet us as far as Appii forum, and The three taverns: whom when Paul saw, he thanked God, and took courage.

16 And when we came to Rome, the centurion delivered the prisoners to the captain of the guard: but Paul was suffered to dwell by himself with a soldier that kept him.

17 And it came to pass, that after three days Paul called the chief of the Jews together: and when they were come together, he said to them, Men and brothers, though I have committed nothing against the people, or customs of our fathers, yet was I delivered prisoner from Jerusalem into the hands of the Romans.

18 Who, when they had examined me, would have let me go, because there was no cause of death in me.

19 But when the Jews spoke against it, I was constrained to appeal to Caesar; not that I had ought to accuse my nation of.

20 For this cause therefore have I called for you, to see you, and to speak with you: because that for the hope of Israel I am bound with this chain.

21 And they said to him, We neither received letters out of Judaea concerning you, neither any of the brothers that came showed or spoke any harm of you.

22 But we desire to hear of you what you think: for as concerning this sect, we know that everywhere it is spoken against.

23 And when they had appointed him a day, there came many to him into his lodging; to whom he expounded and testified the kingdom of God, persuading them concerning Jesus, both out of the law of Moses, and out of the prophets, from morning till evening.

24 And some believed the things which were spoken, and some believed not.

25 And when they agreed not among themselves, they departed, after that Paul had spoken one word, Well spoke the Holy Ghost by Esaias the prophet to our fathers,

26 Saying, Go to this people, and say, Hearing you shall hear, and shall not understand; and seeing you shall see, and not perceive:

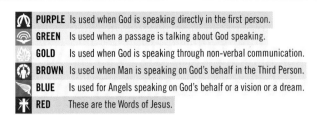

	PURPLE	Is used when God is speaking directly in the first person.
	GREEN	Is used when a passage is talking about God speaking.
	GOLD	Is used when God is speaking through non-verbal communication.
	BROWN	Is used when Man is speaking on God's behalf in the Third Person.
	BLUE	Is used for Angels speaking on God's behalf or a vision or a dream.
	RED	These are the Words of Jesus.

27 For the heart of this people is waxed gross, and their ears are dull of hearing, and their eyes have they closed; lest they should see with their eyes, and hear with their ears, and understand with their heart, and should be converted, and I should heal them.

28 Be it known therefore to you, that the salvation of God is sent to the Gentiles, and that they will hear it.

29 And when he had said these words, the Jews departed, and had great reasoning among themselves.

30 And Paul dwelled two whole years in his own hired house, and received all that came in to him,

31 Preaching the kingdom of God, and teaching those things which concern the Lord Jesus Christ, with all confidence, no man forbidding him.

PERSONAL NOTES

_____

_____

_____

_____

_____

_____

_____

_____

_____

_____

SOME THINGS TO PONDER

1. What sign/miracle made the people traveling with Paul believe that Paul was a god (vs6)? How do you think this affected Paul's testimony among them? _____

_____

2. What other miracles was Paul doing even while a prisoner? What impact do you think these had upon Paul's witness? _____

_____

3. Paul's final words to the Jews were a quote from scripture. What is the message for us today in verses 27-28?

_____

_____

4. How is your heart toward receiving the truths of God? _____

_____

LEARNING TO HEAR HIM - DAY 28 – SUMMARY

MAKE TIME FOR GOD

If you don't make it your highest priority to spend time with God and listen to God, then everything in this world will fill your time and attention. We all battle with the realities of what Jesus spoke of in the parable of the four soils. We struggle with the things of this world and the cares of life, with our own hard hearts and with the unclean spirits sent to harass us.

C.S. Lewis, in a famous book called, "Screwtape Letters," painted the picture of the life of most Christians through the eyes of two demons, Screwtape and his nephew Wormwood, assigned to harass a believer. Screwtape is the senior, experienced demon who gives Wormwood counsel and direction. One of the main assignments is to get the Christian doing good things to keep him from spending time with God.

LISTEN TO GOD EVERY DAY

Many people have had a quiet time most of their life but cannot say they have heard the voice of God. This past fall I spoke with a pastor who loves God and is seeking Him with all his heart but doesn't hear God. I told him to take 30 minutes some time tomorrow to just listen. I told him not to censor what comes to his mind but to just write. I had just left a youth meeting where all but one of the students had heard God speak to them. One of the youth leaders described how he was becoming more aware of the voice of God and the Holy Spirit and was responding to Him. In one week the Holy Spirit had prompted him to witness and to reconnect with an estranged brother.

Most of the hindrances to us hearing God is that we don't listen or that we have a preconceived idea of what it will be like when God speaks. Thus we filter out the promptings of the Holy Spirit and the visions rather than understand that are to pay attention to them.

TRUST & OBEY

Don't fear what God is going to tell you. His main goal is not to make you miserable. If it seems that He is leading you to do something strange, don't rush ahead. Ask for confirmation–first of all, does it agree with scripture? If what you believe you are being led to do agrees with scripture and you pray and get confirmation, then just do it.

It is imperative that you learn to obey the Lord always. You will begin to see the Lord do mighty things in and through your life as you learn to listen and obey Him. He will entrust you with greater things. Don't be surprised if God doesn't have you "doing" anything. He may just tell you that He loves you. He may tell you to just spend more time listening.

BE HUMBLE

Don't boast about what the Lord speaks to you. Don't be surprised if what God speaks to you contrasts with what another hears. For some who always think they are right and anyone who doesn't hear what they hear is wrong, it can become a lonely world. Even prophets would speak what God had told them and leave the results up to God.

One time the Lord had spoken something clearly to me in regard to our ministry. Then the Lord spoke clearly to me to submit to those who opposed what He had spoken to me. Was this a test for me? Were the others led by something other than the Holy Spirit? It wasn't for me to judge that or to know, just to humble myself and obey the Lord. It is challenging to walk "with" others who always are right and cannot humble themselves to say, "It is possible that my own flesh, perspective on life, or something else is clouding my ability to hear God on this."

Right now, my best friend is considering moving to where I live to work and live. It is hard for both of us to know we have heard God on this matter because our own desires to have our families near each other is so great. We both believe it is God, but have both admitted that it could be our own desires.

PONDER WHAT YOU NEED TO PONDER, SPEAK WHAT YOU NEED TO SPEAK

Sometimes God speaks things to us that we are not to share with anyone. God has spoken things to me about another person and told me not to tell the person what He has shown me. Other times He asks me to speak regarding the message He gives to me. God may use you as His mouthpiece to bring a word of encouragement, correction, or direction to someone else. Be sure it is the Lord and give what He speaks to you in humility. Don't add to what He tells you. And speak what the Lord tells you to speak. Leave any results up to the Lord.

You may find yourself on an elevator and God is telling you to tell someone that He loves her or that everything is going to be alright. Do it. You will be amazed at how it will impact that person. You may get something more specific, and it takes courage to obey when you fear that people my think you're crazy. It changed my life one day when someone obeyed God in that way. I had prayed a very specific prayer, that I was willing to go anywhere He wanted but, if He wanted me to stay in Florida, I needed confirmation. I asked him to send someone to walk up off the street and tell me God said to stay. Nothing like that had ever happened to me or anyone I knew. If that happened then I would know God wanted me to stay. Guess what? God sent the most unlikely stranger just four days later with the exact message I had asked God to speak to someone.

I knew God had spoken to him and now I wanted more than anything to know how to hear God. I pray that this study has helped you to learn more and more how to hear God. If it has, please, pass it along to others.

MAKING IT PERSONAL

1. What is the most memorable thing you heard from God during this study? _____

_____

2. How has this study impacted your life? (Please send us your testimony.) _____

_____

3. What are you going to do with what you have learned? _____

_____

DAY 28

DAILY LESSON

WEEK 4 | LESSON 28

TIME TO LISTEN

Write in the space below whatever God may be speaking to you. Don't censor it as you write. If a song comes to mind pay attention to the words and write them. If scripture, write down the reference or the verse, if random thoughts write them. If you see images in your mind write them. Afterward ask God for discernment as to what each thing means.

_____

_____

_____

_____

_____

_____

_____

_____

_____

_____

_____

_____

_____

_____

_____

_____

_____

_____

_____

_____

_____

GOD SPEAKS

LEARN HOW TO HEAR GOD

A JOURNEY THROUGH THE BOOK OF ACTS

SECTION

5

WEEK 5
STUDY GUIDE

GOD SPEAKS

LEARN HOW TO HEAR GOD

A JOURNEY THROUGH THE BOOK OF ACTS

WEEK 5

ACTS 29 - CHURCH ALIVE

Do you ever read novels that are part of a series? It seems like the best series end in such dramatic fashion that you will go out in the middle of the night to the 24-hour store in town to get the next book in the series because you are dying to find out what happens next. OK, I've never been that desperate, but do you know what I mean? You've probably read a series like that before.

Now is the time to let you in on a new chapter in the Bible. Turn to Acts 28:30-31. One of the most incredible books ever written ends like your favorite novel series, wondering what happens next. I believe that God had a purpose in that.

Please don't anyone take me wrong in what I am about to say. I believe God is still writing the Acts of His Church today. Let me clarify for those who just gasped. I'm not saying that any book written today should be added to the Bible. We don't need to add to the canon of scripture.

What I am saying is that the title Acts is a description of the activities that God did through His people, His church, the apostles, deacons, prophets, teachers and more. What else happened to these men? What did God do next? Did God stop acting and working and moving? Did the hero get the girl? All these are questions you tend to be left with.

WHAT IS YOUR STORY LIKE?

God is writing the history accurately in heaven, and one day maybe we can sit down and pick up a volume. How would you like to read the part of the story where you come in? Would it read with all the power, wonder, and drama of the book of Acts in the Word of God? Or, did your God stop working and speaking 2000 years ago?

The beginning of a journey with God that rivals the book of Acts is a personal relationship with a living God. It was meant to be a vital interactive relationship. A relationship involves communication. I know many who have asked Jesus to come into their heart but have

never heard His voice. I hope if that is true of you that this study has awakened this most foundational aspect of your relationship, your ability to listen and hear what God is speaking to you.

God wants to commune with you daily, moment by moment. For that to happen you have to learn to hear Him, and for that to continue, you must obey what He tells you to do. If you stop listening or if He is speaking to you and you choose to ignore what He is saying to you, then you will never experience the drama and power spoken of in this book. Don't worry, you will be normal and fit in with the rest of the crowd. Few press in, listen, hear, and obey to the point where their experience with God ever rivals that of the believers in Acts.

MEDIOCRITY

If you like the easy way then please, by all means, forget everything you learned in this study. Don't take time every day to build a relationship with God, don't listen to His voice, and by all means don't obey Him. Isn't that easy? Mediocrity won't cost you a thing. You will not stand out in the crowd, make anyone uncomfortable or be bothered. Doesn't that sound inviting?

On the other hand, some of you are saying, "Finally, someone is speaking my language!" Some of you are about ready to scream and tear this book to pieces. You have had enough of mediocrity and would give just about anything to experience the Christian life as you read about it in Acts.

For me, it started with listening to God's voice. His Word became so much more alive to me. God began to teach me more and then I began to experience His presence and power like I had read about all my life and never seen in my Christian walk in churches growing up.

If mediocrity makes you sick to your stomach then join the awakening church that is not content anymore with status quo or country club Christianity. Don't be surprised as you learn to listen if some of what God eventually speaks to you challenges you to your core. For me the challenge was immediate.

MY FIRST WORDS

As I began to listen to God He told me to trust Him. There were so few words in those early days but the definition of those two words, "Trust Me," was a manual two inches thick. God was calling me to not take a ministry position or a job, but to seek Him and let Him disciple me. I spent three years with my face in God's Word as a result of that message. As I mentioned earlier I only had one source of finances—whatever God provided, and He did provide.

He would lead me to an inner city church and tell me to sit in the back and watch. He would tell me not to let anyone know I could sing or preach or play guitar but just to watch and listen. He would ask me questions that were hard. Like, "Was that big church you were part of and those fancy ministries you led more important than what is happening here?" Ouch, I knew the answer as I saw these humble servants praying like I'd never seen before and experiencing God's power like I never had.

He showed me humble servants that no one in town knew about who were healing the sick and setting captives free. They worked blue collar jobs or picked up scrap metal and were praying for people all over town and seeing God do miracles. I hungered for that type of walk with God and gladly left behind a much more glamorous experience that was devoid of God's power and sometimes, maybe more often than I would like to admit, even His presence.

GOD IS ALIVE

I have come to realize that there is so much more than what I had known, been taught, or ever believed was possible. God is not silent, hasn't stopped working and is so much more exciting and dynamic than I had ever dreamed. If this sounds appealing to you and you are ready to pay the price of intimacy, listening, obeying and communing with God, then hold onto your seats. This ride could get a little bit bumpy. If you are pregnant, have high blood pressure, or a heart condition, this ride may not be for you. Just kidding! It did seem like

a warning label was appropriate at this point. The cost will be high. He might ask you to talk to that person who is persecuting everyone for their faith like He did to Ananias. He may tell you to go witness to someone of a different nationality like He told Peter when He sent him to Cornelius. Maybe he will send you to sit in the chariot of a ruler and explain God's word to him like He did to Phillip.

If God starts healing people through you, don't be surprised if some religious people want to arrest you, or kick you out of your church—yes, even you pastors. Many pastors have found that as they moved closer to God and experienced His presence, it cost them their pulpit. People around us aren't always excited when we leave mediocrity and truly experience God alive. For some it will be your pastor who is asking you to leave your church. I know this firsthand. Don't worry, God still loves you. Why would you expect your experience to be any different than that of the early church? Stephen was just a deacon, but his message didn't fit the main stream and was really upsetting people. As a result, Stephen paid for his stepping out of the realm of mediocrity with his life.

OK, I just lost some of you. You were thinking of leaving mediocrity till the idea it could cost you your life entered in to the equation. Let me reassure you. It will cost you your life. I guarantee it. Maybe not your physical death but death to normalcy, death to fitting in, death to your comfort and ease and definitely physical comfort, if not your very life. Bye! For those few of you who are still reading, welcome! Welcome to the great adventure. As the great theologian Steven Curtis Chapman once said, "Saddle up your horses, we've got a trail to blaze."

Remember, if you want to read my story, see my book, "The Jesus Training Manual," previously titled, "Lord, Disciple Me." The story doesn't end with the last chapter of that book; God is still writing a great adventure that I get to be part of every single day. The more I listen, the more exciting the journey. As long as I obey His voice I get to be part of the most incredible story ever told. Jump into the book, jump into the journey. I want to pull out your volume in heaven one day and read of your exploits.

GOD SPEAKS

LEARN HOW TO HEAR GOD

A JOURNEY THROUGH THE BOOK OF ACTS

SECTION

6

APPENDIX
STUDY GUIDE

APPENDIX 1

WAYS GOD SPEAKS AND/OR MANIFESTS HIMSELF IN ACTS

Through the resurrected Jesus teaching by the Holy Spirit (Acts 1:1-9; 2:26)

1. Angels (Acts 1:10-11; 5:19-20)

    a.   Two angels spoke when Jesus ascends into heaven (Acts 1:10-12)

    b.   An angel opened the prison doors for Peter (Acts 5:19-20)

    c.   Reference to angels appearing in the Old Testament (Acts 7:35-38)

    d.   Reference to God's law being given by angels (Acts 7:53)

    e.   Angel gave Philip instructions (Acts 8:26)

    f.   Angel came to Cornelius in his vision (Acts 10:3-7)

    g.   Angel came to release Peter from prison again (Acts 12:7-10)

    h.   Angel killed Herod because he failed to give God glory (Acts 12:23)

2. Through Old Testament scripture – Acts 1:16; 2:30-34; 3:18, 21-25; 7:2-3, 30-38, 42-43; 13:32-35, 44-49; 15:15-17; 25:6-7; 26:22-23)

3. By casting lots an apostle was chosen—did God oversee the casting of lots or was this a situation of man using chance and not listening to God? (Acts 1:26)

4. Tongues of fire resting on the heads of the people (Acts 2:3)

5. Speaking in tongues through the Holy Spirit (Acts 2:4, 6, 8-11; 10:42-45)

6. Signs, wonders and miracles (Acts 2:17-20, 22-23, 43; 4:30-31; 5:12; 6:8; 8:6-7)

    a.   Sound of rushing wind (Acts 2:2)

    b.   Tongues of fire over the heads of the people (Acts 2:2-4)

    c.   Speaking in tongues (Acts 2:8-11)

    d.   Many signs, wonders and miracles done by apostles (Acts 2:43)

    e.   God healing a lame man to show Himself (Acts 4:22, 30)

    f.   Peter and John heal the sick (Acts 4:30-31)

    g.   Apostles healed many sick (Acts 5:12)

    h.   Peter being used to heal the sick even by his shadow to show forth God's glory (Acts 5:15-16)

    i.   Steven healing the sick and doing miracles (Acts 6:8)

    j.   Reference to God speaking through the burning bush in the Old Testament (Acts 7:30-34)

k.   Philip doing miracles and healing the sick when preaching and casting out demons (Acts 8:6-7)

l.   Paul and Barnabas preaching in Iconium, accompanied with signs and wonders (Acts 14:3)

m.   Judas and Silas having their message confirmed (Acts 15:32)

n.   God speaking through an earthquake and opening the prison for Paul and Silas (Acts 16:26)

o.   God speaking to us through the resurrection of Jesus to testify that He was the Christ (Acts 17:31)

p.   Paul doing extraordinary miracles in Ephesus (Acts 19:11-12)

7. Prophets

a.   Reference to God speaking through Old Testament prophets (Acts 3:21-24)

b.   Agabus prophesying of a famine that was coming (Acts 11:27-28)

c.   Judas and Silas being shown to be prophets who spoke to the church (Acts 15:32)

d.   Four virgin daughters of Philip prophesying (Acts 21:9)

e.   Agabus prophesying of Paul's imprisonment (Acts 21:10-11)

f.   Paul referencing Old Testament prophets (Acts 26:22-23)

g.   Paul speaking prophetically to those who travelled with him by ship (Acts 28:22)

h.   Paul referencing an Old Testiment prophet (Acts 28:25-27)

8. Preaching through the Holy Spirit (Acts 4:2, 8-12; 11:1)

9. Visions

a.   Steven's vision of Heaven at his stoning (Acts 7:55-56)

b.   Paul's vision of Jesus on the road to Damascus (Acts 9:3-7)

c.   Ananias' vision telling him Paul would come to him (Acts 9:10-16)

d.   Cornelius' vision telling him to go to Peter (Acts 10:3-7)

e.   Peter's vision about the gentiles (Acts 10:10-17; 11:5-10)

f.   Paul's vision of a Macedonian calling him to come (Acts 16:9-10)

g.   Paul's vision where the Lord promised him protection (Acts 18:9-11)

h.   Paul recounting the vision or visitation on the road to Damascus (Acts 22:6-10)

i.   Paul recounting the vision/trance concerning him leaving Jerusalem (Acts 22:17-21)

j.   Paul again recounting his vision, this time to King Agrippa (Acts 26:13-19)

APPENDIX 1
WAYS GOD SPEAKS AND/OR MANIFESTS HIMSELF IN ACTS

10. The Spirit of God speaking directly

    a. Holy Ghost bearing witness to the truth (Acts 5:32)

    b. Spirit speaking to Philip and told him to get in the chariot of the Ethiopian (Acts 8:29)

    c. Spirit speaking to Peter about his vision (Acts 10:19-20)

    d. Spirit telling the church to separate Paul and Barnabas unto the Lord (Acts 13:2)

    e. Paul and Barnabas told by the Holy Spirit not to go to Asia or to Bithynia (Acts 16:6-7)

    f. Paul being compelled by the Spirit to go to Jerusalem (Acts 20:22)

    g. The Holy Spirit speaking everywhere he went that Paul would be jailed and afflicted when he went to Jerusalem (Acts 20:23)

11. A light from heaven (Acts 9:3)

12. Direct visitation of Jesus after the ascension (Acts 9:4-7; 22:14-15)

13. Direct visitation from God (Acts 24:11)

14. In a trance (Acts 10:10; 22:17-21)

15. Preaching by men of God's Word

    a. Peter preaching was by the Holy Spirit (Acts 2)

    b. Stephen preaching by the Holy Spirit (Acts 6)

    c. Paul preaching (Acts 9:27)

    d. Saul and Barnabas preaching in Salamis (Acts 13:5)

    e. Paul preaching in Jerusalem (Acts 13:44-49)

    f. Paul and Barnabas preaching in Antioch (Acts 15:35)

    g. Paul and Silas preaching to the jailer and his family (Acts 16:32)

    h. Paul and Silas preaching in Berea (Acts 17:11-13)

    i. Paul preaching in Corinth (Acts 18:11)

    j. Paul preaching the entire counsel of God in Ephesus (Acts 20:27)

16. Speaking a curse on someone by the leading of the Holy Spirit (Acts 13:9-11)

17. Through giving the Holy Spirit

    a. Jews testified that even gentiles received the Holy Spirit and this was the evidence they needed that God had accepted the gentiles (Acts 15:8)

    b. In Ephesus Paul laid hands on people to receive the Holy Spirit (Acts 19:6)

APPENDIX 2
WHO GOD SPOKE TO IN ACTS

1. The Apostle Luke – God spoke to Luke and, through Luke, wrote the book of Acts.

2. Apostles through Jesus – Jesus spoke through the Holy Spirit to the apostles. (Acts 1:1-5, 8)

3. Tongues of Fire and Speaking in Tongues – The Holy Spirit manifested after Pentecost on those who waited for Him. (Acts 2:2-4, 6, 8-11, 17-20)

4. Through Peter to All Gathered at Pentecost – The Holy Spirit inspired and filled Peter as He preached, illuminating scripture in an extemporaneous sermon. (Acts 2:13-40)

5. Every Soul – The Holy Spirit spoke to people through miracles done by the Holy Spirit through the Apostles. (Acts 2:43)

6. Rulers, Elders, Scribes, Annas the High Priest, Caiaphas, John and Alexander – Peter spoke by the Holy Spirit to those who had arrested them for doing a miracle, causing many to believe in Jesus. (Acts 4:8-12, 19-20)

7. Multitudes Who Believed – There were many signs, wonders and miracles and when they prayed the Holy Spirit came on them and they spoke God's Word boldly. (Acts 4:30-32)

8. Everyone Who Heard of the Mighty Deeds that God Did through the Apostles – People heard about Ananias and Sapphira and of the miracles done by the apostles and it led them to believe in and fear God. (Acts 5:12)

9. Multitudes Who Came to be Healed – Peter and the apostles were healing people, and multitudes came to see, be healed and believe. (Acts 5:15-16)

10. Imprisoned Apostles – Angels came to set them free and commission them to preach and teach in the Temple. (Acts 5:19-20)

11. Those Who Obey – The Holy Spirit witnesses to the miracles and the reality to those who obey God. (Acts 5:32)

12. Multitudes of People and Priests - There was a multitude of people seeing the miracles and hearing the preaching that was by the Holy Spirit; many believed. (Acts 6:7-8)

13. Stephen – Stephen was filled with the Holy Spirit, saw heaven open up, and beheld the Glory of the Father and Jesus. (Acts 7:55-56)

14. People of Samaria – Philip went to Samaria, preached and did miracles, leading many to believe. (Acts 8:6-7)

15. Simon – Simon saw the miracles and believed the words of Philip. (Acts 8:13)

16. Philip – An angel gave Philip directions to go to Gaza. (Acts 8:26)

17. Philip – The Spirit told Philip to go and speak to the Ethiopian in his chariot. (Acts 8:29)

18. Saul and Those with Him – Saul had a visitation from Jesus or a vision of Jesus that was blinding. He heard Jesus speaking to Him. (Acts 9:3-7)

19. Ananias from Damascus – Ananias saw a vision and had the Lord tell him to go to the house of Judas to meet Saul and share the gospel with him. (Acts 9:10-16)

20. Cornelius – A vision from God came and an angel came in the vision to tell Cornelius to send men to Joppa to get Peter to come. (Acts 10:3-7)

21. Peter – God spoke to Peter through a vision to let him know to be ready and to accept Cornelius, a Gentile, and all gentile believers. (Acts 10:10-17)

22. Cornelius' Family, Friends and Others from Joppa and Caesarea—The Holy Spirit confirmed these Gentiles as true believers by pouring out His Spirit on them and through tongues. (Acts 10:44-46)

23. Peter – The Holy Spirit prompted Peter to go with Cornelius. (Acts 11:12)

24. Agabus – God spoke to and through Agabus who was a prophet. (Acts 11:27-28)

25. Peter – God spoke to Peter through an angel that released him from prison. (Acts 12:7-10)

26. Herod – God sent an angel that struck Herod because he failed to give God glory. (Acts 12:23)

27. Prophets, Teachers, Barnabas, Simeon, Lucious and Manaeus in Antioch – The Holy Spirit spoke to them and told them to send out Paul and Barnabas. (Acts 13:2)

28. Sergius Paulus and Elymas – The Holy Spirit spoke a curse on Elymas through Paul because he was coming against everything that Paul was saying. (Acts 13:9-11)

29. Almost the Whole City of Antioch – Scripture tells us that Paul was preaching the Word of God, which is one way that God speaks, and that the entire city came out to hear. (Acts 13:16-41, 44-49)

30. Multitudes of Jews and Greeks in Iconium – Paul and Barnabas and others preached the word of God and did signs, wonders and miracles among them. (Acts 14:3)

31. The People of Lystra, Derby and Lycaonia – Paul and Barnabas preached and did miracles in these cities, spreading God's Word through preaching and miracles. (Acts 14:7, 10)

32. The Counsel of Apostles in Jerusalem – God's Word in the Old Testament was used in the discussion and is a means of God speaking today. (Acts 15:15-17)

33. Gentiles in Antioch – A letter was written by the apostles in union with the Holy Spirit to let the gentiles know that they were free from having to keep the Old Testament Law. (Acts 15:27-28, 32, 35-36)

34. Paul, Silas and Timothy – The Holy Spirit forbid them from going into Asia, and Bithynia. (Acts 16:6-7)

35. Paul – God spoke to Paul through a vision to come to preach in Macedonia. (Acts 16:9-10)

36. Paul, Silas, Prisoners and the Roman Guards – Paul had been arrested and they were praising God and singing hymns in jail when God sent an earthquake that opened the prison doors. Paul then preached the Word of God to all of the people. (Acts 16:26, 32)

37. People of the Synagogue of Thessalonica – Paul preached and taught God's Word to those in Thessalonica. (Acts 17:2-4)

38. People of Berea—Paul and Silas went to Berea and preached God's Word, and the Bereans searched scripture to know if what the apostles said were true. (Acts 17: 11-13)

39. Athenians at Mar's Hill – Paul preached and reasoned with them by the Holy Spirit and presented the commandments of God and the revelation of Jesus' resurrection to them. (Acts 17:30-31)

40. Paul – Paul described being pressed in His Spirit. This is how the Holy Spirit can speak to our human spirit to give direction. (Acts 18:5)

41. Jews in the Synagogue in Corinth – Paul reasoned with them and finally presented Christ to them. (Acts 18:5)

42. Paul – God came to Paul in a night vision and told him to stay in Corinth and that no one would hurt him there. (Acts 18:9-10)

43. Believers in Corinth – Though Paul was not welcome in the synagogue, it's chief ruler and his entire family believed as well as many others, so Paul stayed and taught them. (Acts 18:11)

44. Believers in Ephesus – Paul explained the Holy Spirit, whom they had not understood, to them and they were baptized, received the Holy Spirit, spoke in tongues and prophesied. (Acts 19:6)

45. All who dwelt in Asia – Paul continued to teach for 2 years in this region and did extraordinary miracles so that everyone in the region heard the gospel. (Acts 19:10-12, 20)

46. Paul – The Holy Ghost was speaking in every city where bonds and afflictions awaited Paul. (Acts 20:22-23)

47. Elders at Ephesus – Paul was saying goodbyes, and that he had not failed to declare to them all that God counseled him to declare. (Acts 20:27)

48. Disciples from Tyre – The Holy Spirit spoke to the disciples in Tyre warning them that Paul should not go up to Jerusalem. (Acts 21:4)

49. Four Daughters of Philip – God spoke to them and through them prophetically, though nothing that they said is described. (Acts 21:9)

50. Agabus – The Holy Spirit prophesied through Agabus that Paul would be bound if he went to Jerusalem. (Acts 21:10-11)

51. Multitudes in Jerusalem – Paul told His testimony and the gospel and was taken before the chief council. (Acts 22)

52. Paul – The Lord appeared to him at night and told him not to worry because He was going to also testify of Christ in Rome. (Acts 23:11)

53. Festus – Paul testified to Festus of the gospel. (Acts 25)

54. King Agrippa – Paul shared of the promises of God, of his personal testimony and of Jesus to King Agrippa (Acts 26)

55. Paul – An angel came to Paul in the night telling him that God would save everyone that sailed with him. (Acts 27:22-25)

56. Paul's Sailing companions – Paul gave them the message that God had given him that none of them would die. (Acts 27:22-25, 34)

57. Chief rulers of the Jews in Rome – Paul called for them and testified to them of the gospel. (Acts 28:23-27)

GOD SPEAKS

LEARN HOW TO HEAR GOD

A JOURNEY THROUGH THE BOOK OF ACTS

SECTION

7

RESOURCES

RESOURCES

THERE ARE SEVERAL WAYS TO PARTICIPATE IN THIS PROJECT.

1. Please pray for this project. We are excited to spread the message that God is speaking and we can hear Him. Please pray for favor and financial provision as we move ahead.

2. Begin a Bible Study in your church, life group, or women's/men's group using 'The God Speaks Bible Study." Tell others what you have learned through this study including your pastor, life group leader or Bible Study leader. Share with them how this study impacted your personal relationship with God.

3. Provide us with your honest feedback. You may send us an email at: operationlightforce@gmail.com. If you would like to share with others how this study impacted you please visit our facebook page or facebook fan page under Operation Light Force.

4. You may make a tax-deductible donation to this project and the ministry of Operation Light Force by visiting www.operationlightforce.com and clicking on the "donation" tab. Thank you.

You may visit www.operationlightforce.com or www.godspeaksbible.com

OTHER RESOURCES AVAILABLE AT OPERATION LIGHT FORCE

The Jesus Training Manual

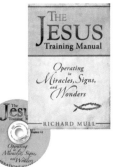

This book is a powerful guide to those things that Jesus taught his disciples and what He would probably teach today. It has impacted the lives of many people.

Lord, Heal Me

Lord, Heal Me is a biblical foundation for healing. It traces God's Word from Genesis to Revelation on the subject of healing. The reader will come to know God as Healer.

40 Day Revolution

The word revolution itself stands for radical change. Campuses are being revolutionized through the power of God's love, prayer, blessing, and serving others in the lives of a "Revival Generation."

OPERATION LIGHT FORCE INSTITUTE

We have developed an extensive training and discipleship resource online. You can learn about your authority as a believer, how to overcome our enemy, how to be healed and minister healing to others. There are downloadable resources, an audio book, eBooks, and more. We also have an exciting and impactful blog that goes out regularly.

Check us out online at: www.operationlightforce.com

God Speaks Interactive Bible

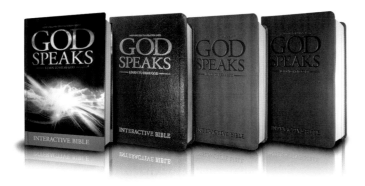

$49 Hard Back Edition (Color)
$94 Genuine Leather (Brown)
$59 Imitation Leather (Tan)
$59 Imitation Leather (Purple)

Unlock the keys to living a supernatural Christian life.

A new Bible that will help you experience a supernatural God speaking to you like never before and will significantly impact Bible reading for a new generation. This book will cause you to expect miracles, hear God, encounter the supernatural, and help you change the world. The Bible has been around for centuries. Many have read the pages but have never discovered it's treasures, never unlocked it's full riches.

What Makes the God Speaks Interactive Bible So Unique?

The God Speaks Interactive Bible traces every detail of God speaking throughout the entire bible. In this Bible everywhere that God speaks is highlighted in 5 colors. The means of designating each of these unique ways of God speaking is through a simple yet meaningful color code. In addition, at the beginning of each book is a list of everyone to whom God spoke in that book. It is inspiring as you see God communicating with people from all walks of life. It will amaze you to see the myriad of ways God has been talking to people throughout history.

Bible Icons and Highlighted Color Coding

	PURPLE	Is used when God is speaking directly in the first person.
	GREEN	Is used when a passage is talking about God speaking.
	BROWN	Is used when Man is speaking on God's behalf in the Third Person.
	BLUE	Is used for Angels speaking on God's behalf or a Vision or a Dream.
	RED	Is used for the Words that Jesus Spoke.
	GOLD	Is used for every Miracle, and all the Acts of God in Scripture.

Interactive QR Codes to link to additional content.

Sample page showing color coding.

{ *Jesus himself said,*
"My sheep hear my voice."
– JOHN 10 }

The God Speaks Bible makes Bible reading new and fresh again, like you've never experienced it before. Order yours today online.

A New Revolution in Bible Reading is Taking Place.

Remember when you first were drawn to the Words of Christ in RED? Now you can see not only the Words of Christ but the Words of Father God throughout the entire Bible. This Bible will help you to learn to hear God better and grow in your intimacy with God, cause you to expect miracles and help you know more how to experience God. You will be amazed how much of the Bible contains direct words from God. Every miracle – all the supernatural found within the Bible has been highlighted for you, and it will astound you.

In this Bible there are resources by Richard Mull, Jim Goll, Mark Virkler, and other great leaders to help you learn how to hear God as He speaks to you, as well as to see the myriad of different ways God still speaks today.

If you need to know how to hear His voice and want to experience a more supernatural life, the God Speaks Interactive Bible will equip you to hear the Voice of God, help you find answers to every question, and lead you to a more powerful and supernatural walk with God.

*www.*GodSpeaksBible*.com*

GOD SPEAKS

SECTION 7: RESOURCES

OPERATION LIGHT FORCE

Light Force Publishing
Seffner, FL 33584
*www.*OperationLightForce.*com*